Contents

Using the Internet in Secondary Schools

Eta De Cicco
Mike Farmer and
James Hargrave

KOGAN
PAGE

YOURS TO HAVE AND TO HOLD

BUT NOT TO COPY

First published in 1998

Kogan Page Limited
120 Pentonville Road
London N1 9JN

British Library Cataloguing in Publication Data

A CIP record for this book is available from the British Library.

ISBN 0 7494 2522 9

Typeset by JS Typesetting, Wellingborough, Northants.
Printed and bound in Great Britain by
Biddles Ltd, Guildford and King's Lynn

Preface

We are in the midst of a dramatic change in the way we communicate with one another across the world. The age of electronic communications is well and truly with us. We can now link networks of computers together, which enable these computers to exchange data. Millions of machines are already linked and the numbers are growing all the time. This is the Internet.

At the present time, there is evidence that more than 80 per cent of UK secondary schools are online, with many of them developing their own school computer networks. Within the next few years, the possibility exists for all secondary school pupils to have regular sustained access.

The speed of technological change means that education often has to make a concerted effort to keep up to date in how best to exploit new technologies for the benefit of learners and those that support them. Although the Internet has been around for many years, easy and friendly access to its gigabytes of data has only come about recently with the emergence of the World Wide Web or the Web, for short.

So what, you say, I can get all that information from other sources. Sure you can! But it's not likely to be as bang up to date as it can be on the Internet and, more importantly, the information is available in a digital format which is readily imported into other packages such as your word processor, spreadsheet or, if it's an image, into your graphics package. This versatility is one of the Internet's major strengths.

The ability of online communications to support every area of the school curriculum is becoming more of a reality. The Internet is important not just as a resource for education but as a communications medium, with a role in keeping teachers in touch with both one another and with experts across the globe. The question for teachers and others involved in the educational process is whether we use these new technologies to replicate existing learning strategies, supported by the conventional classroom, or whether we take the opportunity to redesign teaching and learning methodologies.

It can enhance the teaching and learning strategies offered by teachers. But in order to achieve this, the medium needs to be supported by an organized staff development programme, integrated within teachers' schemes of work, and capable of enabling multiple access.

One thing is becoming more and more clear – when dealing with the Internet, teachers need time. Time to become familiar with the tools, time to look at sites, time to download information, and time to prepare this information so they can use it in the classroom. As anyone who works in education knows, time is a limited commodity as the various demands are made on teachers.

This book attempts to cut down on some of that precious time and bridge a much-needed gap. It will not be covering how to get connected to the Internet or go into great technical detail about computers or software. There are a fair number of books out there that will do just that. So if you're really just starting out, we suggest you put this book aside until you've used the Web for a while, then come back to it later.

Aimed at secondary school teachers, this book will cover Key Stages 3 to 4 of the National Curriculum for England and Wales. In it you will find tested lesson plans, already prepared and used by practising UK teachers, based on materials downloaded from the Internet. All lesson plans will reference the source Web sites and will address specific National Curriculum subjects at the two Key Stage levels.

We certainly don't pretend to solve all the problems teachers face when trying to use the Internet or the Web, but we will certainly do our best to provide guidance, advice and practical suggestions.

Part I

Chapter 1

Tips on using the Web

This book is designed to encourage you to use the Internet in a more productive manner. Although you may have surfed the World Wide Web (Web) already, there's much more to learn about the Web and other Internet (Net) tools. This isn't as hard as it might sound – and in fact it will probably be a lot of fun!

In this chapter we will look at how to make the best use of a Web browser, give some general tips for using the Web and then look at some more advanced topics such as downloading, plug-ins and using the Web 'offline'.

BROWSING THE WEB

Types of browsers

For PC and Macintosh users there are two main Web browsers, Netscape Navigator and Microsoft Internet Explorer. Internet 'addicts' can argue for hours about which one is 'the best' but in fact they are both very similar and do exactly the same thing although in slightly different ways (Figure 1.1).

Both Netscape and Internet Explorer reached version 4 towards the end of 1997 and new versions appear at least once a year (Figure 1.2). However, many people are still using older versions and although these work just as well, they might not handle the newer Web features.

If you are using an Acorn, then you will probably be using the ANT Internet Suite and its ANT Fresco Web browser or Doggysoft's Internet packages. Again, these operate in a similar way to Netscape and Internet Explorer (Figure 1.3).

PC and Macintosh users who don't like the browser that they have on their machine can download another type from the Internet. In

3

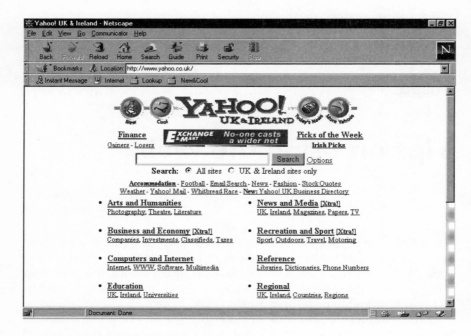

Figure 1.1 Netscape Navigator browser.

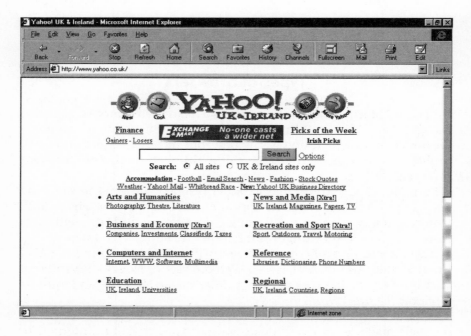

Figure 1.2 Microsoft Internet Explorer browser.

Figure 1.3   ANT Internet Suite and Fresco Web browser.

fact, you can often run more than one browser on your machine. Latest versions and more information about browsers can be found at:

Netscape
http://www.netscape.com
Internet Explorer
http://www.microsoft.com/ie
Ant
http://www.ant.co.uk
Doggysoft
email sales@doggysoft.co.uk

Take me home!

It is quite common to lose your way while surfing the Web. There are so many links to follow and places to go. If this happens, click 'Home' in your browser and you will be taken back to your selected 'Home' page. This is either the Web site of your Internet Service Provider or another page you have selected for yourself.

TIP: You can change the page that you go to when the 'Home' button is clicked.

In Internet Explorer first open the page you want as your Home page in the browser. Select *View* in the toolbar choose *Options* and then the *Navigation* tab. Alter the *Start Page* by selecting *Use Current*.

In Netscape, select *Options* in the toolbar, choose *General Preferences* and then the *Appearance* tab. You will find a box that allows you to alter the Start Up page. Insert into the box the address or URL of the page you'd like to allocate as your Home.

TIP: Sometimes people refer to an Internet site address (for example http://www.bbc.co.uk) as a URL (Universal Resource Locator).

Searching for information

You will need to know how to search for information and this is where search tools come in handy. Part 1, Chapter 2 of this book contains all you need to know about using search tools and getting the information you want from the Web.

Take me straight there

If you already have the URL of the Web site you want to go to, just place the cursor over the 'address' window (in Explorer this is labelled *Address* while in Netscape it is called *Location*), highlight the address that might already be there and replace it with your URL and press return/enter.

TIP: To save time, with most browsers (including Netscape and Internet Explorer) you can key in a Web site address without the 'http://' prefix, for example:

`http://www.cnn.com`

can be keyed in as:

`www.cnn.com`

Help! It doesn't work!

When you click on a link or type in an address, you may get an error message rather than the site that you want. Before giving up, take a look at the tips below.

TIP: When typing in a Web address make sure you copy it accurately, in particular remembering to type lower- and upper-case letters as they are written. For example:

`http://www.abc-project.org.uk/news/index.htm`

will work but if you typed in:

`http://www.abc-project.org.uk/news/INDEX.HTM`

it wouldn't work and nor would:

`http://www.abc-project.org.uk/news.Index.htm`

TIP: The most common error message is '404 File Not Found'. If you type in an Internet address or follow a link and you get this error message or find it doesn't work, try removing the end part of the address, from right to left, until you get to a page that works. For example, you type in:

```
http://www.abc-project.org.uk/news/newspaper/
start.htm
```

but get an error message '404 Not Found'. First of all try:

```
http://www.abc-project.org.uk/news/newspaper
```

thus removing the end of the address. See if this works, if not then try:

```
http://www.abc-project.org.uk/news
```

thus removing the next end part. Continue to remove all the parts on the right-hand side until you find something that works. This is often successful because Web site administrators move the location of files on a Web site but the links pointing to them are not always changed.

If you still can't get the link to work, the site has either changed address completely or is no longer available.

Slow loading pages

If you go to a Web site and it doesn't work or appears very slow to download, first try clicking the *Stop* button on your Web browser and then select *Reload* or *Refresh*. If you still find it impossible, or slow to view, there might be a problem at that site or on the Internet. Try it again later in the day.

If you are using US/Canadian sites, try to access them in the morning. America wakes up sometime after 11.00 am GMT (Greenwich Mean Time) and this results in American and Canadian sites being very busy. You can recognize US sites by their addresses, which usually end in .edu, .com, .gov, .int, .ca and .org.

What's in an address?

You may wonder what Internet addresses mean and how they work. The tip above should provide a clue. Look at the address from the right-hand side and read to the left. The part of the address at the right end is called the *top level domain*. This is usually a country code or alternatively something like .com or .edu.

For historical reasons sites in the USA don't usually have a country code so a site ending in .edu is usually in America. The following Table 1.1 explains some of the more common top level domains:

Table 1.1 Top level domains

Domain	Description
.com	Company
.org	Non-profit organization
.edu	Educational organization
.net	Network resource
.gov	Government organization
.mil	Military organization
.ca	Canada
.uk	United Kingdom
.fr	France
.jp	Japan
.au	Australia
.de	Germany
.nl	The Netherlands

Within some of these top level domains, you get what is known as *sub-domains*. For example, sites ending in .uk also have something in front of this to indicate what sort of UK site it is such as .co.uk. The following Table 1.2 explains the more common UK sub-domains.

Table 1.2 Sub-domain levels

Sub-domain	Description
.co.uk	UK company
.org.uk	UK non-profit organization
.gov.uk	UK government
.ac.uk	UK academic organization
.sch.uk	UK school
.mil.uk	UK military organization
.pol.uk	UK police
.net.uk	UK network resource

Sometimes, using this information, you can even guess the address of an organization's Web page. For example, the BBC's site is:

```
http://www.bbc.co.uk
```

co.uk shows it is a company in the UK. The *www* part of the address is often considered a Web site address and is more a convention than anything else.

Remember that site!

If you go to a Web site that you think you will want to refer to again, you can add it to a list which will facilitate easy access in the future. Netscape uses the term *Bookmarks* and Internet Explorer uses *Favorites* to represent this list but they are both really the same thing.

In your browser, access the page that you want to add and then choose the *Bookmarks* or *Favorites* menu. Click on the *Add to* option. The page's address has now been added to your list of Bookmarks/ Favorites.

If you want to return to that site in the future, just click on the *Bookmarks* or *Favorites* menu and you will see the name of the site listed. Select it with the mouse and your browser will take you there without you having to type in its address.

TIP: You can organize your Bookmarks or Favorites into neat lists under headings therefore grouping similar sites together, for example, *children's sites* or *sport*. This makes sense when you have a lot of sites in your list.

To edit your list in Internet Explorer, choose *Favorites* and then *Organise Favorites*. In Netscape select the *Bookmarks* menu and click on *Go to Bookmarks*.

These instructions may vary depending on the type and version of the browser that you will be using.

DOWNLOADING FILES FROM THE INTERNET

After surfing the Web, there comes a time to move on to some more advanced uses of the Net. In addition to viewing information and pictures on the Net, you can also download them and other files to your computer. Some of the exercises in the curriculum section of the book will require you to download files, including sound, video and programs, and sometimes install and run those programs.

Before starting

Before you download anything to your computer you need to check a few things out. First, make sure that your computer has some sort of *anti-virus* software installed that will protect against downloading files containing viruses. It is very unusual to get a virus with a file downloaded from the Internet, but it is possible. If you do not have anti-virus software you can buy it from a computer supplier or obtain a demo or trial version on a cover disk from a computer magazine or download one from the Internet.

Make sure that the site from which you are downloading looks reputable and is not offering anything that sounds too good to be true. You should be safe downloading from the sites of well-known companies but avoid sites that offer commercial software *free of charge*. Such software might be illegal and the price you pay could be a virus on your computer.

Shareware, freeware, licences

Before downloading programs that you intend to use, check and see if they are free or if you will be required to pay a fee after a period of use.

Many programs available on the Internet are *shareware*. These programs can be freely distributed and tried out on your computer (usually for up to 30 days) but you will need to pay a small fee if you want to *register* the program and continue to use it. Some programs will stop working if you don't pay this fee. Shareware programs should come with information about how you can pay the fee and register.

Several other programs, such as many Web browsers and plug-ins, are made available free to users and no fee is involved. These programs are known as *freeware*.

Finding the right file

If you want to download a particular piece of software or file, then you can search for it. See Part 1, Chapter 2 for more information and tips.

Some sites offer the choice of lots of versions of the same software to download. Make sure the file you choose is appropriate for your computer. For example, if you have a Macintosh, don't choose to download a program that will only run on a PC with Windows 95.

Some files will only work if you have certain hardware and/or software on your computer. For example to play a sound file you will need a sound card and speakers connected to your computer. In addition you may need the correct software for the type of sound you are downloading. The site from which you are obtaining the file should make this clear.

Sometimes you will have to click on boxes and fill in forms before you can download files. You may need to give your name and email address. This is generally safe, and in some cases you will have no choice if you want to download their software (Figure 1.4).

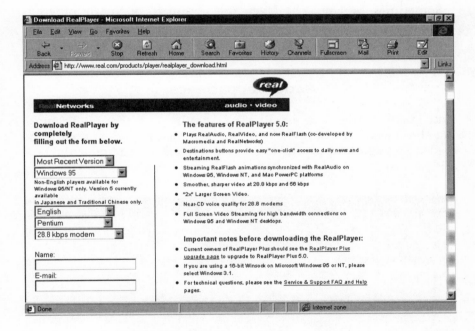

Figure 1.4 Downloading files.

You may find that certain sites give you an option to download from several other Web servers in different parts of the world as well as from their own site. These sites are known as *mirror* sites as they contain a mirror image of the files on the main site.

If given the option, always choose a site as near to your country as you can when downloading files. For example, if there is a site in London and you are in the UK then choose that site, as it will probably speed up your download time.

Where to place files

Once you have located the right file to download, you will need to click on a link to begin the download to your computer. PC and Macintosh users will be prompted with a box asking where you want to save the file and what you want to call it.

The important thing is to remember where you save the file on your computer. Many people create a special directory/folder called *download* or something similar to keep track of downloaded files.

If the computer suggests a name for the file then accept this, otherwise make one up that is meaningful to you. In any case remember and *write down* the name of the file and the directory/folder that you are saving it in.

Sometimes, you may be given the option to open the program straight away rather than save the file to use later. This is a good option if you want to use the program online and not save it for future use.

Patience, patience!

Downloading files can be time-consuming but thankfully most Web browsers give you some indication of the progress of the downloaded files and how much longer it should take to complete the task (Figure 1.5).

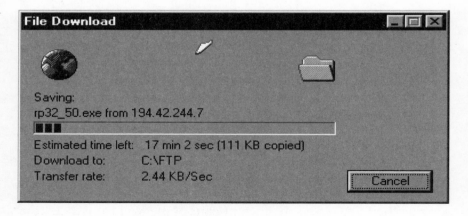

Figure 1.5   Progress indicator.

Problems, problems!

Often downloads progress smoothly without any problems but sometimes you may experience difficulties. If you lose your connection to
the Internet in the middle of a download then sadly you will have to
start again from scratch. This is even the case if 99 per cent of the file
has been downloaded.

Occasionally a download will seem to just stop working altogether
or become painfully slow. If this happens, click on *Stop* in your browser
and try the download again.

If you still have the same problem then try again later as the site is
probably busy dealing with a large number of users. In fact, some sites
limit the number of people that can download at any one time in which
case you will get a message asking you to try again later.

Installing downloaded programs

Once your file is successfully downloaded you may get a message telling
you the download is complete or the download progress box may just
disappear. It is best to close your connection to the Internet at this
point and to close your Web browser and any programs that may be
running.

You now need to locate the program that you have downloaded. Of
course, you wrote down the name of the file and the directory as
suggested earlier. It may be that the file you have downloaded is compressed in some way and you will need to uncompress it before you
can install it. See Part 1, Chapter 4 for more details on the different
types of compression and tools to deal with them.

When you have located the program, double-click on it to begin the
installation process. What happens now will depend on the software
that you are installing. Usually, some kind of install program will appear
and guide you through the installation process.

If not, you may get a black screen and a message about uncompressing
files. If this happens on a PC, then you can look again in the directory
in which you placed the program for another file called *setup* and
double-click on this to complete the installation process. Macintosh
and Acorn users will probably need to uncompress the file first (see
Part 1, Chapter 4). In some cases, you will need to restart your computer
before you can use the program that you have installed.

Plug-ins, sound and video

Web browsers are capable of doing more than just displaying text and graphics. You can also display animated graphics, sound and video. However, to do this, you may need to download a special program that works with your Web browser. These are often referred to as *plug-ins*.

Often a site will tell you that, to view their video or listen to their audio files, you need a particular plug-in and will give a pointer to a location where you can download that plug-in.

To install a plug-in, just follow the instructions on downloading (see 'Downloading files from the Internet', page 9). Plug-ins may be required to complete some of the activities in the curriculum section of this book.

Some of the more common plug-ins are detailed below, together with the site from which you can download them. The latest versions of some Web browsers have the most popular plug-ins already installed.

Shockwave

Shockwave is a very popular plug-in and displays animated graphics and improved sounds. Download if from:

http://www.macromedia.com/

Adobe Acrobat Reader

Acrobat lets you view documents with the original formats intact. This is often used for instruction manuals or government publications. The DFEE (Department for Education and Employment) have used this format to make assessment reports on schools available on the Internet. Download the Adobe Acrobat from:

http://www.adobe.com/

Real Audio/Video

Real Audio/Video lets you listen to live audio and video broadcasts (called *Webcasts*) and also listen to audio/video files as they download (see Part 1, Chapter 3). Download Real Audio from:

http://www.real.co.uk
http://www.real.com

QuickTime

Some sites use QuickTime to display multimedia files. Download Quick-Time from:

```
http://www.quicktime.apple.com
```

Offline browsing

To save time and money, and to accommodate rooms that do not have a connection to the Internet, it is possible to save Web pages on to a disk. This is known as *offline* browsing.

By saving pages to disk, you can avoid any potential pitfalls and dangers that arise from using the Internet live. It avoids problems such as having pupils search for their favourite pop band rather than doing school work or having the telephone connection fail during an Internet session.

The latest browsers such as Internet Explorer 4 allow you to go into *offline* mode and access any Web page that you have visited in the last few days by using the *History* list facility.

You can also obtain more sophisticated offline browsing programs that can download a whole Web site to disk for you to use later. Teleport Pro is available for PC users, whereas Macintosh users could try WebWhacker and Acorn users WebTool (Figure 1.6).

Using an offline browser, you can specify what pages you want and leave the computer to download them. The files will be saved to your hard disk and you can then open them in your Web browser and browse through them.

If you find a *hyperlink* that points to another site that you haven't downloaded, you won't be able to follow this link, but otherwise it works just like being online. Another advantage is that the pages will appear much faster.

Unsuitable material

Most sites on the Internet are perfectly suitable for people of all ages. However, there are a few sites that are certainly unsuitable for pupils and young children as they contain pornography or other unsuitable material.

Some Internet Service Providers offer a special *filtered* service to block access to many of these sites. Alternatively you can obtain special software that blocks sites on your machine, such as *Surf Watch* or *Cyber Sitter*.

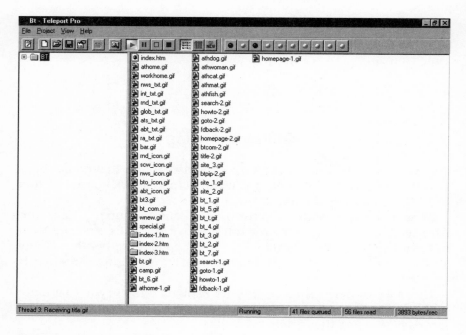

Figure 1.6 Teleport pro.

While these tools are certainly useful and worth investigating, none of them are totally successful and some have the side-effect of blocking perfectly suitable sites and useful activities.

The most effective way to ensure that pupils do not access unsuitable material is to plan adequate adult supervision and to educate pupils about the subject. Make sure that Internet-linked computers are in public places where pupils can be easily seen and supervised.

Many schools require pupils and sometimes parents to sign an agreement before they access the Internet where they promise to adhere to rules regarding the viewing and downloading of offensive materials. As part of the agreement if a pupil breaks the rules, Internet access can be suspended for a period of time or indefinitely.

RESOURCES

Offline browsers

Teleport
http://www.tenmax.com
WebWhacker
http://www.ffg.com/internet.html

WebTool
http://www.ant.co.uk

Software sources

Windows and Macintosh Internet Software
http://tucows.rmplc.co.uk
Acorn Internet Software
http://www.ant.co.uk
General Software
http://www.shareware.com
http://www.download.com
Browsers
http://www.browsers.com

Filtering products and censorship issues

http://www.becta.org.uk/projects/censor/censor.html

Computer pornography

http://www.becta.org.uk/info-sheets/ethics.html

Chapter 2

Tips on searching the Web

SEEK AND YE SHALL FIND

One of the most infuriating features of the Internet is the difficulty in finding the information you want. Imagine searching for information in the world's largest library, where all the books have no covers or titles, are not stored in any particular order and are not indexed in a central catalogue. All right, so this isn't quite the same situation as we have on the Internet at present, but it's close!

In response to this problem, the last few years have seen a growth in search tools, some of which organize Internet resources into searchable subject areas, some of which keyword search documents and others which deliver personalized information to your desktop. If you want to save yourself time and effort, it helps if you can learn how to make the best use of the available search tools. Used correctly, they are a great support in reaching the information you require as quickly and effectively as possible.

However, regardless of the search tool being used, it is far more important to have an effective search strategy. This is true regardless of the type of electronic information you are searching through, whether it is a CD-ROM, library database or the vastness of the Web.

The first step in any information search is to analyse the subject you're seeking. When you're looking for something, it helps to know what it is. Sounds obvious, but there are times when we've all tried to search the Web with only a vague idea of what we're looking for.

Developing your search skills

1. Be clear on exactly what you're looking for. If you're not too sure, use a subject directory first.
2. Think of more than one word that best describes the subject.
3. Be prepared to revise your search words if the first results are not what you wanted.
4. Evaluate what you find.
5. Stay focused.

For example, we want to find out about the writer Shakespeare. Fine! Do we mean we want to learn about the author known as Shakespeare? Or maybe we want to find out what literature he produced? Or view a particular Shakespearean piece? On the other hand, we might want to trace the linguistic origins of the language Shakespeare used? What *exactly* do we want to know?

The most important thing to remember about Internet and Web search tools is that they are constantly evolving animals. No sooner do you think you've got to know a particular search tool when, suddenly, its facilities change. In fact, that's true of the Internet generally. It's a dynamic system where information is added and removed regularly. This can be both annoying and exciting! So just bear this in mind while you're reading the following section on search engines.

GETTING THE BEST FROM THE SEARCH ENGINES

There is no search engine that has an index to the entire contents of the Internet. Each search engine uses different search techniques and builds its index in a different way. These engines use software known as spiders or robots to trawl and index the Web and you'll find that some index every word on every Web page, whereas others only index the headings, subheadings or hypertext links on a page.

So when selecting a search engine, one factor to consider is whether it allows you to specify which part or parts of the document to search. Do you want it to search every word or just look at the headings and subheadings?

Search engines return results, or hits, that most closely match the query made to them. Most engines use frequency – how often the key words you ask it to find appear in a document – to decide how relevant a document is. However, some engines look at both frequency and where those key words are positioned in a document (Figure 2.1).

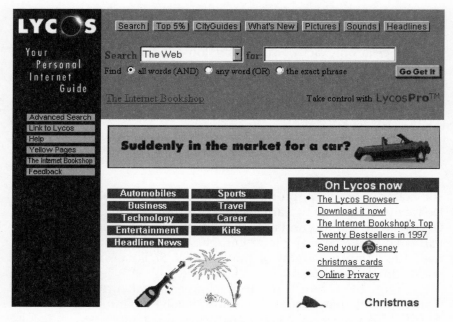

Figure 2.1 The Lycos search engine. © 1994–1997 Mellon University. All rights reserved. Lycos is a registered trademark of Carnegie Mellon University. Used by permission.

Usually the bigger the size of the database being searched, the greater the number of hits you receive, but you might still find that these results are not very useful or relevant. More to the point, even if the search engine does find over 40 000 hits, you're unlikely to have the time to look through them all in detail. Therefore, the way a engine ranks the results is very important. A good, solid results ranking will hopefully mean you'll only need to look at the first 10 or 20 hits.

Given all these variables, it might be a good idea to use more than one search engine to find the information you're looking for. You'll be surprised at how different the results can be for the same search, using the same words, but using different engines. Try it and see!

The Web is not only a large source of information and resources, but presents this information in a non-linear fashion. In the course of your search, you may stumble across and be tempted to view otherwise interesting Web pages, but ones which are patently not relevant to your current search. Unless you've hours to spare, stay on track.

When you receive the results of your search, even if you apparently find exactly what you're looking for, critically evaluate the information. Is it current or well out of date? How can you check its accuracy? Is it intended for a particular audience and therefore biased? Is the source of the information a reliable one?

Tricks of the trade

Search engines are improving all the time but it helps i
their language. This means knowing about words such
operators, wildcards, and keywords.

What's Boolean?

We don't want to confuse matters too much but certain words, referred
to as Boolean operators, are so useful that we really couldn't talk about
successful searches without mentioning at least the most common ones:
AND, OR, NOT and combinations of these. Boolean operators enable
you to make your search more specific by looking for certain words
while ignoring others.

A number of search engines will accept Boolean operators written in
capital letters whereas others will accept them in lower case. Check
out the help and tips' section of the search engine you're using. It will
save time in the long run.

Boolean AND: enables you to search documents that contain two
keywords.

Example:

kids AND software should produce results that contain BOTH
the word 'software' and the word 'kids'.

Boolean OR: broadens your search to include ANY of the
keywords. This is useful for alternative spellings.

Example:

counseling OR counselling.

Note: some engines have as their default – the OR Boolean
operator. So if you type in Tony Blair, you are actually searching for Tony OR Blair.

Boolean NOT: narrows your search by excluding one meaning
of a word.

Example:

alien AND NOT immigrant.

Note: sometimes you cannot use NOT on its own.

Some search engines offer you the choice to use additional operators represented by the words ADJACENT, NEAR and FOLLOWED BY. And to confuse matters even further, there are search tools, like Alta Vista, that let you use the symbols: & for AND, | for OR, ! for NOT, and ~ for NEAR as substitutes for the words.

Boolean words can also be used with curved brackets in order to perform multiple tasks. Using brackets correctly with Boolean operators can greatly increase the efficiency of your search.

Example:

astronomy or space and sun
sun or (space and astronomy)
(sun or space) and astronomy

The first two queries will yield the same results and return documents containing space, astronomy, and sun. If you want the search to find documents containing astronomy and, in the same document, *either* sun or space, you must use the third query.

Example:

not sun and space
(not sun) and space
not (sun and space)

The first two queries are the same and will return documents containing space but not sun. If you want the search for documents that DO NOT contain both sun and space, you must use the third query.

Example:

sun near space and astronomy
(sun near space) and astronomy
(sun near space) and (sun near astronomy)

The first two queries are the same and will return documents containing sun and space, and, in the same document, the word astronomy. If you want the search to find documents containing sun located close to space and, in addition in the same document, the word sun close to the word astronomy, you must use the third query.

Don't worry if you don't get the hang of brackets straight away. Like most things, practice is the solution.

OTHER COMMON SEARCH FEATURES

Wildcards

A wildcard is a symbol that replaces a letter or set of letters. Some search engines do this automatically, but not all. In addition, the symbol used as a wildcard varies between engines; the most common symbols are the star *, and the hash #, but you might find others in use. The ability to substitute wildcards for a letter or set of letters is a useful function as it enables you to find variations on a word.

Example:

educat*

should instruct the search engine to look for words starting with 'educat' like:

education, educational, educated

Case sensitive

Most search engines do not recognize capital letters.

Example:

The difference between Explorer (the space probe) and explorer (a person who explores) might not be distinguished.

Controls

By adding a plus sign '+' or a minus sign '–' in front of a word you are either including or excluding that word in your search.

Example:

+Pinnochio +disney (will find references to Pinnochio and disney)

Example:

+Pinnochio -disney (will find references to Pinnochio but not including disney)

Field searches

The search engine, Alta Vista, lets you restrict searches to certain parts of documents by using a keyword, typed in lower case, followed by a colon and then your search words.

Keywords that can be used are:

title	–	finds documents with the search words in the title
link	–	finds documents that contain at least one link to a page that contains the search word(s)
text	–	finds documents that contain the search word(s) in any part of the visible text of a page
image	–	finds documents with the search word(s) in an image tag. It helps if you search using the two image types used on the Web such as .jpg or .gif (see the example below)
url	–	finds documents with the search word(s) in the page's URL (the page's address)
domain	–	allows you to specify a domain such as fr (for France) it (for Italy) as your search words and it will find documents based on the domain name specified
newsgroups	–	if you know the newsgroup you'd like to search, this is a useful keyword for searching the thousands of newsgroups.

Example:

title: 'The Wall Street Journal'

finds documents with the phrase The Wall Street Journal in the title.

Example:

image:jupiter.jpg

finds documents with any images named jupiter.jpg

Refining searches

A number of search tools enable you to refine your hits. If you find that one of your results better describes what you're looking for, you can ask the search engine to find more sites similar to it.

MORE THAN JUST KEYWORDS

In addition to handling Boolean operators, certain search tools, like Excite, use what they call Intelligent Concept Extraction (ICE), to find relationships that exist between words and ideas. The results of these searches should contain words related to the concepts for which you're searching.

If you look under Chapter 1 'Tips on searching the Web', you will find how to work backwards from the end of an Internet address (URL) until you reach the root directory. This is useful when a search retrieves links to a large number of documents all sitting on one site under one root directory.

Top tips for searching the Web

1. Think about your task before rushing to use a search engine. If you know what general category the information is related to, you can use one of the subject-based tools like Yahoo. Go directly to the topic you think will contain the information you want and see if you find it there. If you are searching for a specific name, use an engine like Alta Vista that uses keyword searches.

2. If you are aware the information you are seeking has several characteristics, such as geographical location or related history, you may find you will need to perform more than one search cycle, refining your search criteria each time round.

3. Commonly used words (such as back, up, from) make poor search keywords. The more distinctive a word, the more useful it will be.

4. Use more than one search engine. Every search engine indexes in a different manner. A keyword may work well with one tool, and badly with another. Try to understand how the keywords you specify relate to the results so with time you can work out how the engine searches.

5. Wildcards are symbols that can represent any character or group of characters in a word. They are useful for retrieving words with different spellings and/or words with a common

---

root (eg flower, flowering, flowered). Symbols used to represent a wildcard vary from one search engine to another, the most common ones being *, #, and ?. For example, to find centre and center, you could search for cent**.

6. If your search produces no results, ensure you've read the tool's help facility, make sure the spelling is right, and if the search tool permits, use Boolean operators. Boolean operators enable you to make your search more specific by allowing you to look for certain words while ignoring others (see section on 'Boolean operators' on page 21). They are represented by the words AND, OR and NOT. Some search engines also use variations on these operators represented by the words ADJACENT, NEAR and FOLLOWED BY. If you still get no results, try to be less specific in your query and use variations on words. If even this fails, use another search engine.

7. If your search produces too many results try again using words that are more unique to what you're looking for. Think of words related to the information you're seeking. Again, search engines that support Boolean logic might be useful here.

8. Bookmark your results page if you think you will be returning to it more than once. Or save it as a source file on your local hard disk or personal area on the server.

9. If you're receiving error messages or cannot make a connection at all, the server may be too busy or temporarily down. Try again after a couple of minutes or wait until a less busy time of the day. Remember to take advantage of world time zones, and use a search engine sited where its local time is not likely to be a busy period.

10. If you get an error message stating that the file cannot be found, that link may no longer exist or the address may have changed. The Internet is dynamic and constantly changing so you may find this is a common occurrence.

TOOLS OF THE TRADE

The following search engines are divided into four main types:

- subject directories
- search engines
- meta search tools
- specialized search engines.

Subject directories

Subject directories are hierarchically organized indexes categorized into subject areas. They are usually compiled by humans, or have some human intervention, and many include a search facility to enable you to search the categories. For a broad topic, use one of these subject directories first. For more specific information, try one of the Search tools that use keywords and Boolean operators.

As the content of the Web is constantly changing, sites come and go. Many of them move addresses. A subject guide compiled by a subject specialist is more likely to pick up on these changes and therefore produce more up-to-date relevant returns.

Such guides exist for virtually every topic. The databases of subject directories tend to be smaller than those of the search engines but are useful for searching for a general subject, rather than a specific item of information.

The first starting place is the Argus Clearinghouse, which offers a guide to many of these specialized directories:

Argus Clearinghouse
http://www.clearinghouse.net/

Examples of subject specific directories are:

Galaxy
http://galaxy.tradewave.com/
Global Online Directory
http://www.gold.net/gold/indexdir.new.html
Identify
http://www.identify.com
Internet Public Library
http://ipl.sils.umich.edu:80/ref/ref/
Magellan
http://www.mckinley.com/
Nerd World
http://www.nerdworld.com/
The Otis Index
http://www.otis.net/index.html
Search.com
http://www.search.com/
World Wide Web Virtual Library
http://www.w3org/hypertext/DataSources/bySubject/
Overview.html
Yahoo
http://www.yahoo.com/

Search engines

Search engines are best used for conducting keyword searches. Each differs in its search speed, interface, display of results and the amount of help it offers. Engines also differ in the manner in which they search (Figure 2.2).

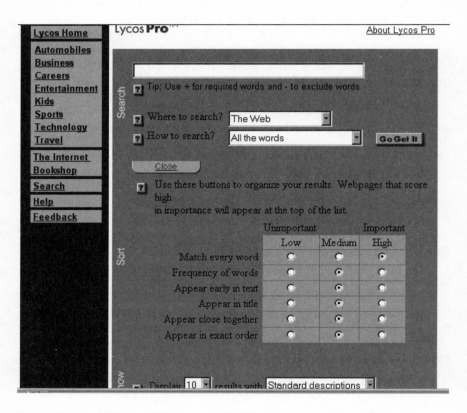

Figure 2.2 Advanced features of different ways of searching an engine. © 1994–1997 Carnegie Mellon University. All rights reserved. Lycos is a registered trademark of Carnegie Mellon University. Used by permission.

Most search engines index every word of a document and since those words might be found in an inappropriate context, this often means you get a large number of results but not all of them relevant. Others allow you to restrict your search to headings, subheadings or other particular parts of the document. The majority retrieve documents in order of decreasing relevance.

Examples:

Aliweb
`http://web.nexor.co.uk/public/aliweb/search/doc/`
`form.html`
Alta Vista
`http://altavista.digital.com/`
EuroFerret
`http://www.muscat.co.uk/ferret/`
Excite
`http://www.excite.com/`
Excite – UK version
`http://uk.excite.com/`
G.O.D.
`http://www.god.co.uk/`
HotBot
`http://www.hotbot.com/`
Infoseek
`http://www.infoseek.com/`
Lycos
`http://www.lycos.com/`
Lycos UK
`http://www-uk.lycos.com/`
OpenText
`http://search.opentext.com/`
REX
`http://rex.skyline.net/`
WebCrawler
`http://webcrawler.com/`
World Wide Web Worm
`http://wwww.cs.colorado.edu/wwww/`

Meta search tools

These search tools allow you to search multiple databases simultaneously via a single interface. There are also sites available that collect the different search tools in one place. They do not offer the same level of control over the search as the individual search engines, but their response time can be fast. Many meta tools can now sort results by site and type of resource, and some allow you to decide which search engines to include.

Examples:

Aesir
http://www.aesir.com/aesir/staff/JimSearch.html
All 4 One
http://all4one.com/
Dogpile
http://www.dogpile.com/
Find It
http://www.itools.com/find-it/find-it.html
Inference Find
http://m5.inference.com/ifind/
isearch UK
http://www.isearch.co.uk/index-n3.html
Meta Crawler
http://www.metacrawler.com/
Pro Fusion
http://www.designlab.ukans.edu/profusion/
Savvy Search
http://guaraldi.cs.colostate.edu:2000/form/
Search.com
http://www.search.com/

Specialized search engines

These are search engines that cater for very specific subject areas.

Achoo – Healthcare
http://www.achoo.com/
Aqueous – Water Related
http://www.aqueous.com/
BigBook – US Businesses
http://www.bigbook.com/
Cinemachine – Movie Reviews
http://www.cinemachine.com
DejaNews
http://www.dejanews.com
Netmall – Goods and Services
http://www.netmall.com
Motherload – Web Directories and Search Engines
http://www.cosmix.com/motherload/

SHAREWARE.COM – Software
http://www.shareware.com/
Sports Directory – Sports
http://www.sport-hq.com/
Yahooligans – a site specifically for children with its own search engine
http://www.yahooligans.com/

UK-BASED SEARCH ENGINES

Since it can be quicker for UK users to access sites in the UK, here is a list of search engines, divided into the subject directories, search engines and specialized tools, available in the UK.

Subject directories

Examples:

Yahoo UK
http://yahoo.co.uk
Yellow Pages UK
http://www.yell.co.uk/

Search engines

Examples:

EuroFerret
http://www.muscat.co.uk/ferret/

Meta search tools

Examples:

isearch UK
http://www.isearch.co.uk/index-n3.html

Specialized search engines

Examples:

ADAM – Architecture, Design and Media
http://www.adam.ac.uk/
EEVL – Edinburgh Engineering Virtual Library
http://eevl.ac.uk/
OMNI – Medical
http://omni.ac.uk/
SOSIG – Social Sciences
http://sosig.esrc.bris.ac.uk/

Searching – the wish list
You want an overview of your topic from the general to specific.

Try Yahoo

You want to just browse general categories such as Science, Health and Medicine, Education.

Try Galaxy, Magellan, Yahoo, Yellow Pages

You want to do a precise search because your terms are not very broad.

Try Alta Vista, WebCrawler, Infoseek, Lycos

You want a small number of hits with excellent summaries and then be able to order them so that the ones most useful to you are displayed first.

Try Excite, Alta Vista

You want to be able to use natural language in your searches, that is, real sentences.

Try Infoseek

You want to search the major databases and integrate the results.

Try MetaCrawler

You want a search tool containing descriptive reviews of sites.

Try Magellan, WebCrawler

You want a fast, powerful tool that enables you to use common words likely to appear in many documents and to be able to refine your search criteria.

Try HotBot

You want to search an event by its date.

Try HotBot

You want a search tool that recognizes and allows for capital letters.

Try Infoseek, Alta Vista

You want a search tool that recognizes proper names.

Try HotBot

You want to be able to search by Internet domain name (ac, org, com, etc).

Try MetaCrawler, HotBot

You want to search for a piece of art, a photo or an image.

Try Infoseek Imageseek, Lycos Media

You want to find designs, logos, videos, or music.

Try HotBot

You want to trace the exact words of a quotation or an author.

Try OpenText

You want to see a site just for young people with its own search engine.

Yahooligans

You want to search archives of UseNet post. UseNet is especially useful if you are looking for items related to computers, the Internet, science, sociology, psychology and hobbies.

Try Reference.COM, Deja News, Excite

THE MOUNTAIN COMES TO MOHAMMED

Internet and Web developers are always looking for easier ways of delivering the information you want to your desktop. Searching the Web using search tools requires you to make the effort to connect to the Net, find a suitable search engine and construct an appropriate search query. New technologies, often referred to as personalized Web sites, intelligent agents, or push/pull technologies, are intended to save you time and effort by automatically sending the information you require direct to your computer.

Search engines such as Alta Vista, Yahoo and Excite lead the way in the field of personalized Web pages, although there are other examples, such as Open Sesame. My Yahoo is one example of an extensive customized Web site that can be altered to reflect your tastes. Just answer a few questions about your lifestyle – music, recreation, shopping and other interests, and from then on, whenever you go to the My Yahoo site, only information pertaining to *your* interests are displayed. This type of personalization still requires you to make the effort to link to the relevant Web site.

If personalized Web pages don't offer you enough, you could always try intelligent agents. Intelligent agents is a term used to describe programs that act like a search engine, only they allow you to get on with other tasks as they roam the Internet to find relevant information. Autonomy's Agentware is an example of this technology.

Autonomy's software enables you to create 'agents' on your computer. You allocate an agent for every topic of research and the theory is that the more you use them, the more these agents learn about your topics and therefore yield increasingly accurate results. Gradually, you can build up a library of information based on your areas of interest.

Finally, there are the push technologies. These can be likened to traditional broadcasting insofar as information is regularly delivered to you, one-way, direct to your computer. My Yahoo News Ticker is a fine example of this new technology. It uses the preferences set up in My Yahoo to create 'channels' (note the broadcasting terminology) that automatically download information and display it, news-ticker style, on your desktop.

Microsoft and Netscape, producers of the two most popular Web browsers, are heavily investing in push technologies. Netscape are offering Netcaster as the software that enables you to subscribe to 'channels' whereas Microsoft offer the opportunity to subscribe to various 'channels' as an integral part of their Web browser Internet Explorer (version 4).

Other push software to look out for is the PointCast Network, Marimba's Castanet Tuner, and BackWeb. If you want regular software downloads, you need to use Castanet, Netcaster or BackWeb. If you don't want to confine yourself just to the content providers offered with a particular push software, with IE and Netcaster you can also subscribe to Web pages. In this way, updates to your favourite Web pages are downloaded to your desktop.

Current push programs can take over your desktop and eat up system resources. If you like the idea of having information delivered straight to your desktop, check out whether the push client lets you schedule downloads or timetable searches for updates at a given time.

For those of you with only limited time on the Net, Netcaster's 'push' capabilities allow you to schedule downloads and view them offline when you have the time. For those with a permanent link to the Net, it enables you to receive constant information updates in the background while you are working on other tasks. The downside is that a push client will slow down your machine.

Push technologies are currently geared to the consumer market and are dominated by the USA. This is unfortunate for Internet users in the UK as many of the items that appear on customized Web pages relate to US news, shops, music and education. Likewise the various push technology 'channels' tend to deliver mainly US-orientated information. However, as the technology becomes more robust and prevalent, this may very well change.

RESOURCES

Open Sesame
http://www.opensesame.com
My Yahoo
http://my.yahoo.com
My Yahoo News Ticker
http://my.yahoo.com/ticker.html
Agentware
http://www.agentware.com/main/agent/index.html
Netcaster
http://www.netscape.com/comprod/products/communicator/
netcaster_frameset.html
Internet Explorer v4
http://www.microsoft.com/ie/download
PointCast
ftp.corp2.pointcast.com/pub/pcn16m.exe
Castanet
ftp.download.com/pub/win95/internet/castuner20.EXE
BackWeb
ftp.simtel.net/pub/simtelnet/win95/inet/bw20.zip

REFERENCES

Barlow, Linda (1997) *The Spider's Apprentice – Tips on Searching the Web.*
http://www.monash.com/spidap.html
Evaluation of Selected Internet Search Tools (1997).
http://www.library.nwu.edu/resources/internet/search/
evaluate.html
Notess, Greg R. (1997) 'Comparing net directories', *Database* **20** (1),
61–4.
http://www.onlineinc.com/database/FebDB97/nets2.html
Sullivan, Danny (1997) *A Webmaster's Guide to Search Engines and Directories.*
http://calafia.com/webmasters/
Tillman, Hope N. (1997) *Evaluating Quality on the Net.*
http://www.tiac.net/users/hope/findqual.html

Chapter 3

Designing Web pages for schools

As mentioned in Chapters 1 and 2 we have looked at how we can use the Internet to find and use information. In particular we have focused on the World Wide Web. We're going to continue to focus on the Web in this chapter but will be learning how to use the Web to publish information for ourselves!

One of the great things about the Internet is that it gives everyone the chance to be a publisher! On the Internet anyone can publish (more or less) whatever they like!

This chapter is not going to tell you in full detail how you can author Web pages as this depends a lot on the type of computer and software you're using. However, it does provide some useful tips to help get you started and pointers to gain more information.

You don't need a great deal of experience to write Web pages for yourself (see below) but you will need to be familiar with what the Web is and have used it for a short while. If you've read the first two chapters and had a 'surf' then you should be ready!

HTML AND ALL THAT!

Don't let anyone tell you that Web pages are 'too hard' for you to do or that you need to be a programmer. Anyone can write Web pages these days! You may hear people talking about a mysterious thing called HTML (Hyper-Text Mark-up Language). This is the language that Web pages are written in and looks something like this:

```
<HTML>
<HEAD>
<TITLE>This is my homepage!!!</TITLE>
</HEAD>
<BODY>
<H1>Welcome to my homepage!!</H1>
<B>This is in Bold!!</B>
<I>And this is in Italics!</I>
</BODY>
```

This 'code' would produce the following Web page (Figure 3.1):

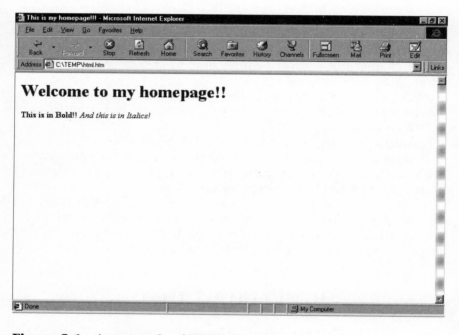

Figure 3.1 An example of HTML language.

You might well have noticed that HTML works by putting <tags> around text that alters its appearance. For example, putting a <B> tag in front of text makes it **bold**. The tag </B> ends this and text following the latter tag is no longer in bold.

TIP: You can look at the HTML of a Web page that you have displayed in your browser. In Internet Explorer choose *view* and then *source*. In Netscape choose *View* and then *Document Source*.

This is quite simple to learn but there is some good news if you use a PC or a Macintosh. To write Web pages, you don't need to learn HTML. As you will see in the section on 'Web authoring software', page 44, there are several programs that can write the HTML for you, leaving you to concentrate on the fun bit, designing your pages.

BEFORE STARTING WORK

Before you actually start work on your Web site it's worth considering a few important points to save extra work later on!

Why?

Before doing anything at all think about why you are setting up the Web site, what is the purpose, audience, etc. The following section may help you to decide what a school Web site is for and why it's a good idea to have one.

Web sites set up because everyone else has one are usually quite obvious, so put some thought into why you need a Web site before starting!

Planning

Decide on a plan for your Web site before you start constructing your pages. You may wish to sketch it out on paper first – you might want to draw a diagram showing all the links between pages on the site.

Audience

Think about who will be looking at your pages – pupils, parents, other teachers – and then make the pages appropriate to the intended audience.

WHY HAVE A WEB SITE?

At the end of 1997 well over 1000 schools in the UK had Web sites, ranging from a single page saying 'under development' to several hundred pages of information. All these schools obviously thought that setting up a Web site was a 'good idea'.

Historically, the first schools to have their own Web sites did so because it was a new technology. The purpose of the site was simple; it was for the sake of having a Web site and because so few schools had Web sites it was a success just to set one up (Figure 3.2).

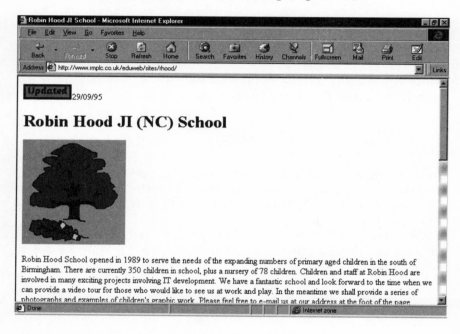

Figure 3.2 Early stages of a World Wide Web Site.

The reasons for setting up a Web site for your school are different.

MARKETING YOUR SCHOOL

About two to three years ago, universities were in a similar situation to schools today. Several had Web pages, but many did not. Some of these universities were understandably reluctant to set up pages without a good reason. However, those universities that already had Web sites began to use them to publish information about their courses and saw an increase in applicants as a result (Figure 3.3).

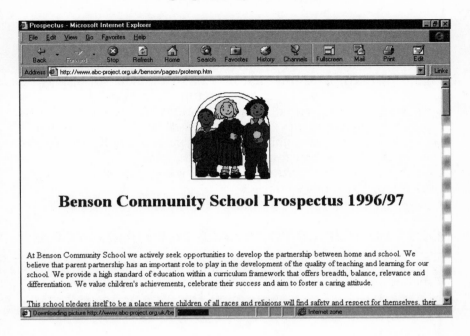

Figure 3.3 A Web page as a marketing tool.

This situation has not yet happened in schools. However, more and more people have access in one way or another to the Internet and 'marketing' is becoming a major reason to establish a site.

PROVIDING YOUR OWN INFORMATION

If you do not yet have a Web site, you may be interested to type in your school's name to a search tool and see what you find. Chances are that the first 'hits' will be links to your school's OFSTED (Office for Standard and Testing in Education) report and to the DFEE (Department for Education and Employment) performance indicators about your school. These are all freely available and the range of information is slowly growing.

As well as this information about your school you may well decide that you would like to provide your own information from a school's point of view.

Remember that more and more people will be turning to the Internet to look for information when choosing a school for their children or even where to apply for a job.

THE ULTIMATE DISPLAY BOARD

Information that you make available on your Web site does not have to be for marketing reasons. You may be in the habit of displaying pupils' work on the wall in school. The Internet makes it possible for pupils' work to be viewed all over the world. This in itself can be an incentive for achievement. Pupils often work hard when they know that their work is to be published online, particularly if provision is made for any feedback such as using email.

You can easily use a scanner or digital camera (see page 46) to put work on to the school's Web pages.

GET THE PUPILS TO DO ALL THE HARD WORK!

Key Stage 3 and 4 pupils should be quite able to produce Web pages for themselves after some teaching in the basics of HTML (Figure 3.4). If you use a package such as Microsoft FrontPage or Adobe PageMill producing Web pages is as straightforward as using a word processor.

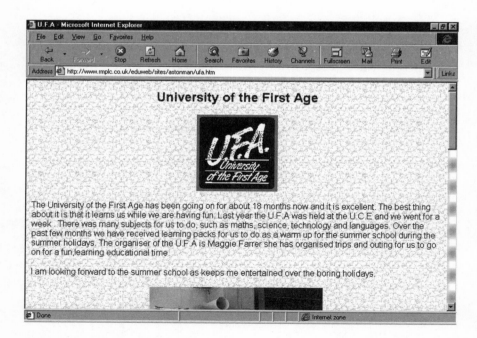

Figure 3.4 A pupil's page.

Pupils might put information about their own work and/or interests online or be entrusted to take part in providing the more 'official' information about their school. A professional-looking site created by the pupils themselves would make a more impressive site than a 'flash' site designed by a public relations company.

TOOLS FOR THE JOB

You will need a certain amount of hardware and software for Web page authoring. Make sure that you have everything ready before you start.

Essential – computer (obviously!), modem, Internet account with some Web space, graphics manipulation software, text editor, Web browser.
Useful – Web authoring software or word processor, scanner, digital camera

---

Computer

You will not need an all-singing and dancing latest specification computer for constructing Web pages, but as Web page construction usually involves work with graphics and some multi-tasking, a computer which has a reasonably fast processor would be advisable.

Using a PC, the minimum specification is a Pentium with at least 16Mb of RAM running Windows 95. Macintosh users should aim for a PowerPC or Performa.

Modem

Some computers have a built-in modem. If this is not the case, then you need to buy one that has a speed of at least 28.8 Kps. Kps is an abbreviation for kilobits of data transmitted per second.

Internet account and Web space

To publish your Web pages you will need to be able to upload them to the Internet. The method used to do this is referred to as FTP (File Transfer Protocol) (see Part 1, Chapter 4). This stores your pages on a Web server that is permanently connected to the Internet.

Unless you already have a Web server at school, you will need to pay for an account with an Internet Service Provider (ISP). However, the good news is that almost all dial-up Internet Service Providers such as Research Machines (RM), Demon, Virgin and America On Line (AOL) provide some space for your Web pages on their servers either free or at a nominal fee. If you already have an account ask them for details, and if you are just setting one up make sure you check how much space is available. Usually 5Mb of space is quite enough.

Web authoring software

If you are using a PC or a Mac then you might like to consider programs such as Microsoft FrontPage to construct your Web pages (Figure 3.5). Both of these work in a similar way to a word processor and are WYSIWYG (What You See Is What You Get). Although these programs make the construction of Web pages easier some knowledge of HTML is required.

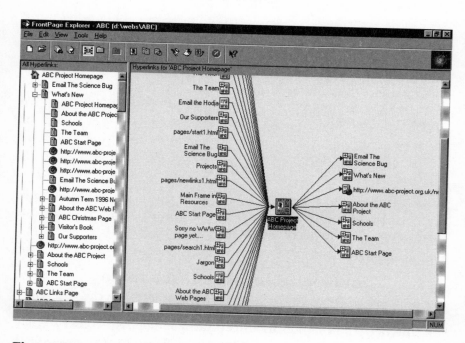

Figure 3.5 Microsoft Frontpage.

Information about Microsoft FrontPage can be found at:
`http://www.microsoft.com/frontpage`

Information about Adobe PageMill can be found at:
`http://www.adobe.com/prodindex/pagemill/main.html`

Acorn users will need to write their Web pages in HTML and can look at the following Web site for more assistance and the latest software:
`http://www.ant.co.uk`

Before you start with your school's Web site find out as much as you can about the different authoring software.

There may be courses in your area that might be useful or you may know someone who has already designed Web pages who could help you.

Graphics manipulation software

Graphics Software is useful to convert Graphics files into the GIF and JPEG formats that are used in Web pages (see 'Graphics', page 48). Microsoft FrontPage already comes with a program called Image Composer otherwise you could use shareware such as Paint Shop Pro if you are using a PC.

You can download Paint Shop Pro from:
`http://www.jasc.com`

These programs can help you to manipulate images that you have on your computer or input with a scanner or digital camera. For example you could resize a photograph that you scanned into your computer so that it would fit in the right place on your Web page.

Scanner

A Scanner allows you to scan photographs and drawings into your computer and is very useful for Web page construction. You can scan photographs of the school, pupils, teachers, etc and also any work that the pupils have produced.

If you must choose one accessory for Web construction then a scanner would be the most useful purchase and would also be helpful in many other areas of the school's work. Make sure you buy a flatbed A4 scanner and check that it will connect to the computer that you are using.

Many scanners use the 'SCSI' interface (Small Computer Systems Interface) and is pronounced 'scuzzie'. It is the name given to a type of interface that connects an accessory (such as a scanner) to your computer.

If you are using a PC you might need to open the computer to fit an expansion card. If you are not happy doing this, or want to use the scanner on more than one PC, then choose a scanner that plugs into the parallel port (printer port) of any PC. Most Macs have SCSI interfaces built in and you should just be able to plug the scanner in.

Digital camera

A digital camera is similar to an ordinary camera but allows you to take a picture and then input it directly into a computer without the need to get the photographs developed or scanned using a scanner.

Since digital cameras are still fairly expensive, you can always get a similar and indeed usually superior quality effect by taking photographs with a conventional camera and scanning them into your computer.

However, if you are getting pupils to produce their own pages and want quick results, then a digital camera would be a good investment. And it might also be useful for other purposes.

SITE DESIGN

Most Web sites have a consistent 'look and feel' throughout the whole site. Graphic designers and big companies call this 'corporate identity', but for a school site this might mean all the pages having the same colour background with the school logo on them! Some Web authoring programs allow you to save a page as a 'template' so that all the pages that you base on the template will look the same (eg colour of text, background colour).

It's worth taking the time to sort out the basics of site design before you start work as it's much easier to get right from the first page!

Colour

Think about the colours of your pages. You may wish to use the same background and text colours on all pages, or use different ones for each page. If you do decide to use background images or colours, then make sure that the text is still readable against the background colour and that the link colours are appropriate.

Title

Make sure that each page has a proper title and one that reflects the page's content. The title is important because when you have a site with many pages you will need to be able to distinguish one page from another.

Page ownership

Put your name and the date you last updated the page on each page. When completing dates, it is best to write them out in full (eg 1 May 1997) rather than use shorthand (1/5/97) as this means different things in different countries. If you have one, include an email address on every page so users can feed back comments about your site.

Contact details

Make sure that at least one page on your site contains full contact details for your school, such as name, address, telephone/fax numbers and email address. It is amazing how many Web sites neglect to include even a telephone number! When placing phone numbers online, you might want to include them in the international format since some of your site visitors might be calling from outside the UK:

0121 123 1234, becomes:
+44 121 123 1234

It is probably best to include telephone numbers in both formats as many UK callers might be confused by the international format.

Spelling and other errors

Make sure that you check the document for spelling and other errors before putting it on the Web. This is particularly important for school pages as it looks dreadful to potential parents and visitors if words are spelt incorrectly.

Speed of access

Remember that many people still use slow modems to access the Web so huge graphics and lots of the latest bells and whistles may look good on your machine but not so good on an old machine using a 14.4 Kbps modem!

Browsers

Though the HTML language is supposed to be a standard, the two main browsers, *Microsoft Internet Explorer* and *Netscape Navigator,* often display the same page in slightly different ways. This situation is further complicated by the fact that different versions of the same browser (eg Netscape 2.0 and Netscape 3.0) also display quite differently. It is a good idea, therefore, to try viewing your Web site in both of these browsers and in different versions so that you can see the image that potential visitors to your site might experience.

Page size

In general, design your pages to work at 640 × 480 screen resolution with 256 colours. Screen resolution is measured in 'pixels' which are just dots of light on a screen. Most 14" monitors are set to work on 640 × 480 pixels, most 15" monitors work at 800 × 600 pixels. The screen resolution affects the size of images on the screen and how much information you can see at once. You may also like to check images at a higher screen resolution (eg 800 × 600) to see if they work.

Screen length

Avoid pages that are longer than 2–3 computer screens in length. Divide a long page into more manageable 'chunks' and put links to these pages from your very first page – known as the Home page.

GRAPHICS

Web pages look good with graphics on them, but there are a few tips that will help to ensure that the graphics do not deter visitors from reading the page. This can happen when it takes forever to download thus spoiling the effect!

Size of graphics files

Avoid huge graphics files, or if you want to include them, use 'thumbnails'. Thumbnails are simply smaller versions of a larger graphic that are displayed by the browser in place of the larger image. They can be created in a graphics package by resizing the image.

The smaller 'thumbnail' images (Figure 3.6) are then made into clickable links to their larger versions (Figure 3.7) and give the user an idea about what the images are like before downloading them. In general, graphics should be no larger than 40–50K (kilobytes).

GIFs and JPEGs

Try to use the GIF file format for line drawings and the JPEG file format for photographs. GIFs and JPEGs are just different sorts of compressed graphics files. For example an image of say 100K can be reduced in size by compression to about 30K. The main advantage of using compression is to reduce the overall size of Web documents so that they download much faster.

Progressive loading of graphics files

When given the option, save GIF and JPEG files in 'interlaced' or 'progressive' file formats. This means that the viewer will see the image emerging bit by bit as the graphic downloads. Otherwise, you will have to wait until the whole image is downloaded to the screen before viewing it.

Width of images

Make sure the width of graphics files fit into the 640 × 480 screen resolution that many people still use. Set your monitor's screen resolution to these settings and check out your pages before making them available to your intended users for viewing.

ALT tag

The ALT tag is part of HTML script and consists of words that are displayed by the browser as an alternative to the graphic itself. If you looked at the HTML you would see something like this:

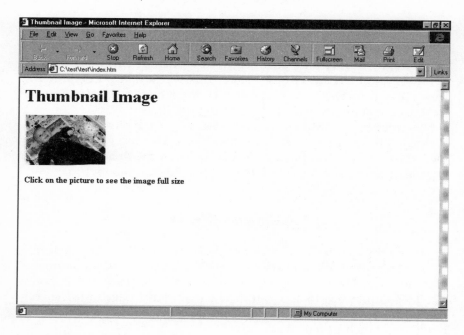

Figure 3.6   Thumbnail image.

[IMG SRC='happy.gif' ALT='Picture of Smiling Face']

This would show the graphic called happy.gif on Web browsers that can display graphics, or the text 'Picture of Smiling Face' on text only browsers.

It is a good idea to go to the trouble of putting a meaningful description of any images you are using in with the ALT tag.

Where to find graphics

As well as images that you scan or produce yourself, you might also want to use ready-made graphics on your Web site. Whenever using an image produced by someone else, pay special attention to copyright (see 'Copyright', page 54). There are several sites on the Web that exist just to provide graphics for Web sites. You can find these by using a search tool or visit the site:

http://www.clipart.com

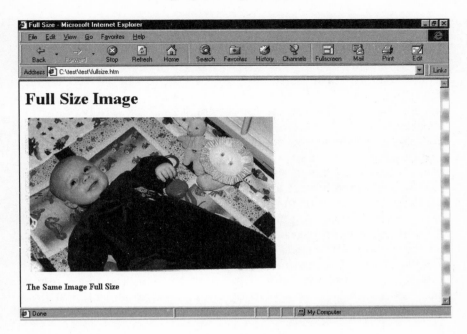

Figure 3.7 Larger version of thumbnail image.

This site contains links to many sources of either free clipart or ones for which you pay a small fee. You may also be able to buy images on CD-ROM, but again be very careful to check that you are allowed to use these online.

For more help on downloading from the Web, see Part 1, Chapter 1 of this book.

Animated GIFs

You may sometimes find pages that have animated graphics on them. These are usually 'animated GIFs'. If you would like to use simple animation on your pages, then you can create your own using a specialized program or alternatively, download animated GIFs from the Web.

Do a search using the keywords 'animated GIF' in a search tool (see Part 1, Chapter 2) and then download the images as explained in Part 1, Chapter 1 of this book. Again, make sure that you are allowed to do this first (see 'Copyright', page 54).

LINKS

When the World Wide Web first started, it was based on the idea of hypertext links, those underlined words that can be clicked on and which then lead to other Web pages. Nowadays, it's not only words that act as hyperlinks. You can enable graphics and a variety of navigational aids, such as forward and backward buttons, to lead to other Web pages. Whatever you do, try and place a link back to your Home page on every page on your Web site.

When creating links to another site or within your own site, check that the links actually work and keep checking them at regular intervals, as any future alterations may cause the links to stop working. Certain Web page authoring programs (such as *Microsoft FrontPage*) can check all the links between pages on your site, and even links on your pages to other people's Web sites.

However, avoid including too many links to other people's sites on your pages as other users might jump on to these and never return! Many sites avoid this problem by concentrating all external links together on a single 'links' page.

Keeping up to date

Remember that people will find your site boring if it never changes. Keep it up to date! In particular, if the site promises newsletters or other similar items then make sure these are actually added. People will not appreciate seeing news concerned with the spring term at the end of the summer term! If you need to keep 'old' information because some of it is still relevant, then plan for part of your site to act as an archive.

It might also help to have a 'What's New' page so that regular visitors to your site can quickly see what has changed since their last visit. As mentioned before, always check your links to ensure that they are still working.

Making it interactive

One of the great things about Web pages is that you can encourage interaction. For example, you might be able to send an email message to the author of a page, fill out an online form, or even complete a knowledge quiz and have your score displayed almost immediately.

Whereas advanced interactive pages might include a Visitor's Book (Figure 3.8), where your visitor fills out an online form and the results are posted to the site, thus keeping the book automatically updated,

Figure 3.8 Visitor's Book.

similar online forms might enable the user to request a prospectus, ask for other information or even register for an online discussion group.

Adding multimedia

When Web pages were first invented, they often consisted of just plain text files with a few hypertext links. However, it was not long before graphics were added and now most Web sites make use of both text and graphics to make the content more interesting and easier to navigate.

The latest Web sites are making use of sound and video to enhance the presentation of the pages. In fact, it is even possible to 'webcast' live events, such as concerts and to listen to radio stations.

When sounds and video were first added to Web pages they were often in a format specific to certain types of computers (ie .WAV files for PCs or .QT files for the Macintosh (see Part 1, Chapter 4). These had to be downloaded to the computer before the sound or video could be played.

Recently, a new technology known as 'streaming' has been introduced which means that sound and video can be heard or seen as it is being downloaded to the computer. The best known implementation of streaming sound technology is called Real Audio. A disadvantage is that, in addition to needing a sound card and either speakers or head-phones attached to your computer, you must have a Real Audio 'plug-in' installed on your machine.

The latest Web browsers often have a Real Audio plug-in installed for you, but if your browser does not, then you can download the plug-in by visiting the Real Web site at:

```
http://www.real.com
```

Refer to Part 1, Chapter 1 of this book for more general information on downloading plug-ins.

Copyright

Many people think that the usual rules of copyright do not apply on the Internet but this is not the case. When producing pages, it is essential to ensure that you either own the copyright to the material you are publishing yourself or that you have obtained the consent of the copyright owners before publishing it.

It is important to remember that images you may see on other people's pages cannot just be copied and used on your page without consent. In fact, in some cases, even the owner of the site from which you downloaded the resources may not have permission to use them! Be vigilant!

There are some sites that specifically allow you to download and use their resources on your pages. However, sometimes they ask you to put a link and/or a credit to them on your pages and you should always do this when asked. You should proceed as if publishing the document in more conventional formats and not let the ease of downloading and copying other people's files from the Internet get you into trouble online!

Responsibility for Web page content

It is usual for a school to appoint one person to be in overall charge of the Web site. This ensures that there is consistency in the look and content of all the pages!

It would be wise to get the permission of the headteacher before starting work on a site and to ensure that he or she sees the pages before they are published. Some schools have formed small working groups to provide and update content on their pages.

It is particularly important if you are allowing pupils to create Web content to check its suitability for public viewing before publishing it online. Remember that people will judge your school from the content of its Web pages!

Child protection

When using pictures of pupils on Web sites, you may wish to obtain the consent of parents in advance if this is something that the school would normally do when publishing pupils' photographs elsewhere.

It is sensible not to include the full name of a child or any other information that might identify an individual pupil. If pupils maintain their own personal Web pages and are including photographs of themselves, ensure that they avoid revealing their full names or any other personal details online. Encourage them to use first names only (eg, 'My name is Sarah and I am in Year 9') and to practise caution.

If your site offers the facility for visitors to send email messages directly to a pupil or group of pupils, then it is important to make sure that a teacher checks their content. It is better to be safe than sorry where a pupil's online safety is concerned. More information about these issues can be found in Part 1, Chapter 1 of this book.

FTP – Getting your Web files on to the Internet

One of the most confusing parts of publishing a Web site is the process of transferring the Web files that you have produced on your own computer to a Web server (computer). The Web server might be that of your Internet Service Provider (ISP) or one maintained at your own school. You do this using a process known as File Transport Protocol (FTP) (see Part 1, Chapter 4).

In order to connect to your Web server, you will need to know some basic information such as the Internet address of the Web server, and a username and password provided to you by the Web server administrator. This is sometimes the same as the one you have for email and logging-on to the Internet, but you would need to check this with your ISP or, again, with your Web server administrator. Once you have uploaded your files on to the Web server, check that they all work correctly by using your Web browser to go to the Internet address of your pages.

Adding your pages to search engines

Now that you have published your pages on the Internet, remember that unless you do something about it no one will know that they are there or where to find them. It's a bit like having a new telephone line connected! Until you tell people the number or list it in a directory, no one will know they are there!

All the major search engines have pages where you can submit a new Internet address. You can usually find these on the Home page of the relevant search engine (see Part 1, Chapter 2). There are also some sites online that can help you list your pages, such as:

```
http://www.submit-it.com
```

These may want you to pay for more advanced publicity services. Finally, don't forget to include the Web site address of your school on letterheads, newsletters and other correspondence.

RESOURCES

The Web itself is a great place to look for information on Web page authoring. Use a search engine such as Yahoo to look for the keyword HTML. Some of the following links might be useful:

A beginner's guide to HTML
```
http://www.ncsa.uiuc.edu/General/Internet/WWW/
HTMLPrimer.html
```
A beginners guide to HTML programming
```
http://members.aol.com/teachemath/class.htm
```
Bare bones guide to HTML
```
http://werbach.com/barebones/
```
Craigs 1 stop for HTML
```
http://www.cyber-quest.com/home/craig/index.html
```
HTML crash course
```
http://www.w3-tech.com/crash/
```
HTML made really easy
```
http://www.jmarshall.com/easy/html/
```
HTML: An interactive tutorial for beginners
```
http://www.davesite.com/Webstation/html/
```
Top 15 mistakes of first time Web design
```
http://www2.dgsys.com/~hollyb/top15.html
```
Teach me! HTML
```
http://www.geocities.com/Athens/Forum/4977/index.html
```

Chapter 4

Other useful tools

In Chapters 1–3 we talked about the Internet predominantly as a source of information, a place to go and find, retrieve and save valuable resources. This is an important function of the Internet, particularly the Web. However, it can play other roles too! Further useful functions include:

- supporting collaborative working practices
- providing the opportunity for schools to publicize themselves to a global audience
- allowing staff and pupils to harness the power of electronic publishing.

Chapter 3 has already provided some information on the use of the Web as a publicity and publication medium for schools. This chapter will concentrate on collaborative working and then examine a range of other Internet tools. It is important here to remind readers that this book is not for beginners, but is intended for users who already have some experience of the Internet and the Web.

COLLABORATIVE WORKING

Collaboration is a form of communication, but one that is often focused on a specific aim and is time-limited. It is a way of people networking and working together on a particular task or project.

Electronic communications technologies are a powerful way of enabling collaborative working at a distance. They can bring together individuals from different organizations in different locations and provide them with the tools to work together as a group.

Electronic networks have the advantage of making available new information almost instantaneously. Transmitting information in a digital form allows individuals and groups to find, send, receive and store large amounts of data.

However, collaborative working does not just happen because you have a number of people each with electronic access to one another. By taking time to assess current or planned collaborative working, you might save yourself and your school some major headaches in the future. Before plunging into online collaboration, it might be worth a few minutes to ask yourself and your school managers a few of the following questions.

Online or not online?

1. Would the cost of travel put attendance of meetings beyond the means of all or some of the participants?
2. Are there deadlines that electronic collaboration could help you meet quicker and more easily?
3. Is there one participant willing to act as a facilitator? Would the facilitator be willing to spend the time to manage the collaborative process electronically?
4. Is the technology easily accessible to all the participants? Can collaboration occur effectively with only a few key participants working online?
5. Will training for participants be required? How long will this take and how much will it cost?
6. Who will provide technical assistance?
7. Can the nature of the discussions and collaborative process be captured electronically and archived?
8. Will the technology be mainly text-orientated, and if so, will this communication medium be a barrier for some participants? Can this barrier be overcome?

Collaborative working of any type is more successful if one member of the team is designated as the facilitator. Online collaboration requires not only the presence of a facilitator, but the added requirement that all participants make use of their online facilities regularly. So if email is the method of communication selected, participants should check their email often and respond to those messages requiring action.

The more widely spread the participants geographically, the less opportunity there is for face-to-face meetings and the more important the role electronic networking could play. Information and communications technologies are often successful in supporting already existing relationships between individuals, groups and organizations but they can also encourage otherwise disparate strangers to communicate and share information.

SO HOW DO YOU DO IT?

There are a number of tools you can use to collaborate online. One method is our good friend the electronic mail (email) system. Although never really developed as a conferencing tool, a versatile email package like Eudora or Pegasus, both available as shareware (you pay a nominal fee) or as professional packages (costing you a commercial fee) will make an adequate start. Equally, browsers like Netscape Navigator offer email as part of their facilities (Figure 4.1).

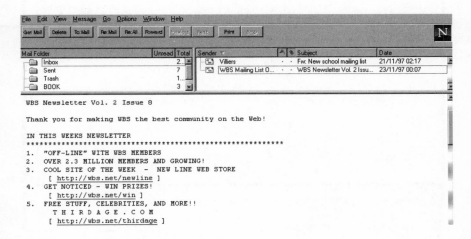

Figure 4.1 Netscape's email facility.

Another method is a dedicated group conferencing package such as FirstClass. A dedicated system usually contains all the features necessary to support online conferencing such as email, the ability to archive messages into separate folders, bulletin boards, file sharing, and real-time text-based interactivity. Real-time means you communicate with other individuals who are 'logged' on to the FirstClass system at the same time as you are.

Finally there are Web conferencing tools which can be accessed via the Web itself. Use one of the search engines and take a look at some of them.

You may decide to opt for one of these choices, or for a combination of all three. But first, let's take a look at each of these options, starting with the simplest tool — electronic mail.

Electronic mail

Internet electronic mail (email) is a method of sending a message to either an individual or to a group of individuals. Email is much like sending a letter via the postal services to a specific address – you can send an email to anyone on the Internet who has an Internet email address (Figure 4.2). You don't even need to be using the same Internet Service Provider as the recipient.

Mail

From	Subject	Received
HotFlash	HotFlash 4.47 – Bolster the Butler	Sun Nov 2 7:31 am
James Hargrave	Web Page construction Section	Wed Oct 29 1:02 pm
my-yahoo@yahoo-inc.com	Registration confirmation – My Yahoo!	Wed Oct 29 12:48 pm
Eta De Cicco	vc final txt documents and print	Tue Oct 28 1:21 pm
Coola	NC World by e-mail!	Tue Oct 28 7:44 am
news@wbs.net	WBS Newsletter Vol. 2 Issue 7	Sat Oct 25 12:56 pm
Matterform Media	HTML Grinder and Theseus upgrade	Fri Oct 24 6:38 pm
listmaster@calafia.com	SE Report #11, Part 2 of 2	Tue Oct 7 12:10 am
listmaster@calafia.com	SE Report #11, Part 1 of 2	Mon Oct 6 6:09 pm
eta_de_cicco@ncet.org.uk	videoconferencing directory – UK	Tue Sep 23 12:51 pm

Mail	10 Messages	
Mailbox	148 Messages	
Outbox	0 Messages	
Sent Mail	98 Messages	
Wastebasket	2 Messages	

Figure 4.2 Example of an email inbox showing messages received.

The speed of delivery is one important benefit of email, but there are others. Using email offers you the opportunity to overcome the limitations of time, and can be more economical than equivalent alternatives. Basically, you can communicate with others in different countries, even those in different time zones, for the cost of a local telephone call and the subscription charges of your Internet Service Provider. You send messages when it is convenient for you and the recipients can pick them up when it's convenient for them.

In addition, it is possible to send one or more messages to a group of people in one single operation. Most modern email packages have a facility that enables you to create your own group addresses. Each group contains the email addresses of selected individuals, and you can often add and remove names from the group. This makes it much easier and quicker to communicate with a large number of people.

The downside to email communication is that it cannot guarantee privacy. Internet email can be read by *any* system administrator of any of the computers that handle the message on its way to your desktop. Although it's unlikely that someone will pick your message out of the thousands of email that flow through computers, you can never be absolutely sure. So unless you are using reliable encryption software, never write anything in an email you wouldn't mind being broadcast to the world.

Equally, do not assume that your email has been delivered to its destination, or that it has been read. Email may fail to be delivered for any number of reasons: the recipient's computer dealing with email (the email server) may be down, you may encounter broken connections along the way or you might have made an error when typing in the email address. Even if it should arrive on the recipient's desktop, never assume it has been read. Unless you know that the individual you are emailing reads his or her email regularly, always allow for the fact that not everyone has either instant or constant email access.

Tips for making best use of email

- Email should be checked regularly – at least once a week, daily if possible.
- Email messages should be kept short. Long messages are harder to read on a computer screen. If the document is a long one, and your email package has the facility, send the document as an enclosure/attachment.
- Email is more suited to informal communication and is highly conversational.
- Try and stick to one single issue in each email message otherwise people will tend to get confused between the different threads of conversation.
- Email depends mainly on text to convey meaning. Emotion and tone of voice are lost. There are conventions that attempt to overcome this handicap. Try and familiarize yourself with them.
- Keep copies of any important messages you send for your own reference or in case they either fail to arrive safely and you need to resend them.
- Email is never completely secure, although encryption software can help.

Finally, modern email packages give you the facility to send attachments or enclosures with your message. These can be any types of file – a text document, a piece of software, a sound or picture file, or even a movie. However, there are some factors you have to take into consideration when sending files via email.

You will find that attaching files means they will be encoded, as this is the only way email can deliver different types of files electronically. There are different email encoding standards, or protocols, and these depend on what type of computer the sender and recipient are using.

The most common protocols are *binhex* for the Macintosh, and *MIME and Uuencode* for both the PC and Acorn machines. If your email package cannot automatically deal with these different encoding types, you may find that you'll need additional software on your machine to 'translate' the files. You can search for these additional pieces of software on the Web using one of the many search tools (see Part 1, Chapter 2). Often, with the more recent email packages, an email message will state, as part of its message, what type of encoding has occurred (see below).

Example of a MIME email message:

Message for Eta De Cicco
From: James
Date: Mon, Jul 21, 1997 12:06 pm
Subject: Mime Messages
To:

*********************** NOTE ***********************
There may be important message content
contained in the following MIME Information.
****

– – – – – – –MIME Information follows – – – – – – –
– – – – – – – –

This is a multi-part message in MIME format.

– – – – – – –25E460E01AB9
Content-Type: text/plain; charset=us-ascii
Content-Transfer-Encoding: 7bit

<<<<<< See above 'Message Body' >>>>>>

– – – – – – –25E460E01AB9
Content-Type: text/html; charset=us-ascii
Content-Transfer-Encoding: 7bit

> Content-Disposition: inline; filename='t101.html'
>
> Eta,
>
> Mime is a method of encoding that is used to send text and other types of files, such as pictures, sounds or software, via email. If your email package can't read this file, you'll need to have separate software on your machine that can decode it.
>
> regards,
>
> James
>
> --------217255D267B4--

You may find that certain Internet Service Providers set a maximum file size limit on both the size of the message and the size of any enclosures. Certain files, particularly pictures and movies, can be very large and have to be *compressed* in order to make them smaller, easier and quicker to transmit. Again, you need separate software on your computer that can both compress and uncompress files. If the file is still too big, even when compressed, and the recipient has access to file transfer protocol (FTP), FTP the file (see FTP).

Finally, you need to make sure that those receiving your attachments have either the same make of software you used to create the file, or another package that can handle that type of file. For example, if you used Microsoft Word to create the text file you emailed over, the recipient will usually either need to have the same version or a more recent version of Microsoft Word *or* another package that can read Word files. If you used Microsoft Excel to produce a spreadsheet, the recipient will either need the same or a more recent version of Microsoft Excel *or* another package that can deal with Excel files to look at the spreadsheet.

Well, that's the complicated bit out of the way. Now let's briefly mention email rules. Yes, there are such things and they have developed over time to make email messages easier to use and understand. They are quite simple but very effective. The most common rules of etiquette are described in Figure 4.3.

Because email correspondence tends to be asynchronous (not read by the reader at the same time as the message is written), you need to give the recipient a context in which to read the message. So what do we mean by context? Let's compare the three examples below.

Example I

Sounds fine by me.

Being rude	Capital letters are CONSIDERED TO BE SHOUTING! Unless you intend to shout or be impolite (not recommended), don't use capitals!
Emotions	Since email doesn't convey emotions very well, symbols have emerged that represent different moods and feelings. These are known as smileys. Examples: J — happy or smiling ;-) — joking or winking L — unhappy or sad.
Quoting	When you respond to a message, the sender may not remember their exact words in their original email to you and be confused by your reply. To avoid this, it is customary to quote the part of the sentence or paragraph of the message to which you are responding before replying.
Subject	Try to give the recipient a good idea of what your email is all about by giving your message a clear subject title. Often the title is all they have to go on when deciding whether to read your message immediately, later or not at all.
Acronyms	Email messages are often written in an informal manner. Over time, acronyms have developed to express the most common sentences and expressions. The most common are: BTW — By The Way FYI — For Your Information IMHO — In My Humble/Honest Opinion TIA — Thanks In Advance RTFM — Read The Manual ('Manual' here refers to any documentation) LOL — [I] Laughed Out Loud [at what you wrote] ROTFL — [I am] Rolling On The Floor Laughing [at what you wrote] RSN — Real Soon Now

Figure 4.3 Examples of the most common email conventions.

This email really tells the recipient very little. Your reply might be a response to one of hundreds of messages they have sent out recently – or not so recently! Unless they remember exactly what you are agreeing with, it would take them some time to trace their previous email to you and reread it. It would be much better if you provided some context for your reply:

Example II

>so I was thinking we might meet up Friday 22nd at 2.00pm.
Sounds fine by me.

The '>' is one of the conventions for quoting someone else's words. It reminds your reader of what was written in the last email and is followed by your reply. You should include just enough content to provide a context for the reply and no more. You can even quote back two or three different parts of someone else's message, each with a separate reply.

Example III

>Have you talked to the English Department about those CD-ROMs
>we discussed at the staff meeting?
>Yes. They were keen to go ahead and order them. I'll let you have
>the budget code when I next see you.
>I thought the document you sent me was very interesting, particu-
>larly the section on integrating
>videoconferencing in classroom practice.
>Agreed. I think we ought to set up a presentation and demo of the
>system at the next staff meeting.

As you can see, by providing context for your replies, the email not only makes more sense, it is easier to read and assimilate. And your recipient will thank you for it.

Using email as a collaborative tool

Positive points: email is the simplest and easiest approach to collaborative working. It is often the cheapest option and email packages can function quite adequately on a low specification computer. It is particularly good for short-term projects with a small group of people.

Negative points: email does not lend itself to organizing messages into topics or threads of conversation. It cannot be easily archived and the process becomes difficult to manage when you have a large group of people involved, with numerous email messages being sent to participants.

Mailing lists

Mailing lists sprang up from the need to exploit email's ability to post electronic messages to a group of people. Those who participate in a mailing list often share a common interest. A participant sends a message to one email address only, and that message is then redistributed to every mailing list member. The mailing list can be either fully automated (maintained by a computer) or operated by a person (who might manually collect and redistribute the messages).

The advantages of mailing lists over traditional methods such as mail merges and long-distance faxes is the considerable reduction in costs, the speed of delivery and the fact that material arrives in a digital format and can therefore be easily customized. By participating in a mailing list, people who share a common interest can engage in discussion or seek advice and help from other participants. Mailing lists and newsgroups (see page 66) are a very good source of expertise on particular topics and can often help participants solve particular problems.

The benefits of mailing lists and newsgroups are the ability to engage in discussion of specific issues, tap into expertise and experience, and share information. The downside is that subscribing to mailing lists can generate many messages, often swamping your email account. In cases like this, it might be useful either to use an email package that can filter messages or check if the mailing list has a *digest* version. A digest collects all the messages together over a given period of time, often a month, and organizes them by topic with an index. If even this is too much for you to read and absorb, consider temporarily suspending messages to your email account or unsubscribing from the list all together. Both options are often offered by mailing lists.

You can find a comprehensive list of email discussion groups and instructions on how to subscribe to them on the Web:

```
http://www.liszt.com
http://www.mailbase.ac.uk
http://catalog.com/vivian/interest-group-search.html
```

Mailing lists can be archived and organized in such a fashion that any specialized and expert content could be made available not only to participants of the mailing list or newsgroup (see 'UseNet', page 69), but to anyone with an interest in that topic. One important fact to remember is that email still depends mainly on text to convey meaning. It's very easy to offend individuals accidentally by, for example, writing what you intend to be a funny, joking comment but which is received as criticism. Conventions have developed that attempt to overcome this handicap. Try and familiarize yourself with them if you don't want to get *flamed*. Getting flamed means you receive either harsh, inflammatory responses or actual personal attacks via email.

Fortunately, technology keeps on moving forward and although email packages are still predominantly text-based, already voicemail software is being developed that can deal with audio as well as text, and some packages can even embed images and movies in the body of the message.

Closed conferencing

If you would like more versatility when engaged in electronic collaboration, you might want to experiment with dedicated conferencing packages. These give you many more functions than email but are often *closed* systems, that is, they can only communicate with individuals who have the same conferencing software *and* who have permission to use the computer where the conferencing discussions and information is kept. Passwords are used to keep intruders out.

Within the conferencing system FirstClass, for example, you can set up numerous discussion topics – each with its own area for messages and basically acting like giant bulletin-boards. First you go online and download the most recent messages in the topic areas that interest you. Then you prepare your replies offline and when you're ready, go back online and place your messages in the topic areas for others to pick up and read later. Easy really! Messages and comments can be archived allowing you to see how a discussion on a particular topic has progressed, or maybe you want to start an entirely new topic. It's up to you!

Conferencing packages also offer email facilities, but usually only to those who have permission to use the system. Like Internet email, you can attach files to your messages but unlike Internet email, you'll find that the recipient can open the attached files easily without bothering with decoding or decompressing them. That's because they're using the same software as you are.

Since dedicated conferencing packages are produced to encourage collaboration and communication, you will find that they offer details about other users who are on the same system as yourself. You can look at another user's biography, his or her email address, and sometimes even his or her photograph.

Even more impressive, Web-based conferencing software is starting to emerge which provides the added benefit of the Web's multimedia environment to the discussion process. Web conferencing software acts like a dedicated conferencing system in that topics can be arranged in logical order, user details can be provided (with the added bonus – or is that embarrassment – of photos, video or sound clips?), and past discussions can be archived. A very basic collaborative tool NetMeeting, which comprises of video, audio and a whiteboard facility (a shared work area), is already available with the Microsoft browser Internet Explorer and both are *free* to educational users.

Finally, there are videoconferencing (audio and video) packages that can operate over the Internet. CUSeeMe and Dwyco Video Conferencing are examples. Naturally, they are in their infancy at present, and the quality cannot compare with even desktop videoconferencing systems, but it's a start. As they improve, they may provide another avenue for collaborative working across the Internet.

Who knows? We might find that, in the not too distant future, we shall be able to communicate via a combination of Web conferencing and videoconferencing systems that use audio, visual, text and other multimedia.

Other uses of electronic networking

Electronic networking can be utilized in a couple of other important ways. You can transfer data, such as examination results, payroll information or statistical data from one location to another, thus saving time and effort. Some colleges of further education are already sending statistical information to their funding councils electronically and school examination details are being transferred to and from local education authorities. In addition, using the technology can result in staff gaining or improving their research, graphic arts and communication skills therefore contributing to their overall computer literacy.

TALK! TALK! TALK!

Collaborative working is all very well, but there are times when we would like to communicate with like-minded individuals without necessarily working with them on a project or topic. In cases like these, bulletin-boards and UseNet newsgroups are useful facilities.

Bulletin-boards

Electronic bulletin-boards are much like non-electronic public notice-boards but instead of pinning up messages on a notice-board, you post electronic messages to a bulletin-board that is then publicly visible to anyone who has access to it. Bulletin-boards need not be available on the Internet, in fact, many of them are not and you have to dial into them. All you need is appropriate *software* to access the bulletin-board, a modem and a phone line.

You will find that the majority of bulletin-boards are free to join while others will require you to pay a subscription fee. Not only do they hold messages, they are a great source of Public Domain (freeware or shareware) programs and information which can be either of a general or specialist nature. Files held on a bulletin-board are often compressed so you'll need to know about the different compression formats (see 'Squeezing it all in', page 76) to take full advantage of them.

Unfortunately, certain bulletin-boards can also hold many files that are considered to be 'unsuitable' for pupils. Often these bulletin-boards require a subscription and declaration of age before entry is permitted. However, pupil access to bulletin-boards should still be approached with the same awareness as when dealing with any other public electronic network (see Part 1, Chapter 1) – with caution and care.

UseNet

Bulletin-boards vary in size with some only holding less than a dozen discussion topics, others many hundreds. UseNet requires software known as a *Newsreader* to access a server (computer) that carries UseNet groups. The newsreader can be either held on your own computer or on the server which carries the UseNet service.

When you first take a look at UseNet, you could be faced with over 5000 topics, known as newsgroups. These newsgroups cover discussions on subjects as varied as television soaps, dyslexia, cookery, computer operating systems and much, much more. Newsgroups can be an excellent source of expertise and information. Equally, they can be a source of gossip, misinformation and downright dribble(Figure 4.4)!

When you first join a mailing list or access a newsgroup, it would be wise to look at its FAQ (frequently asked questions). The FAQ file might be included in the 'Welcome' message you receive when you first subscribe or available by request from the mailing list. This FAQ file contains all the questions a new entrant (newbie) is likely to ask about the mailing list or newsgroup.

Do try and read it first as nothing irritates other regular users than a newbie asking basic questions about the list or group that is contained in the FAQ. Once you've read the FAQ, lurk for while. Lurking is when you just read messages for a time without replying to them. It's a good way to get to know whether the group you've joined meets your needs and ensures you don't post messages that are inappropriate to the group.

News Server		Unread	Total		Sender			Subject	Date
⊞ uk.comp.* (8 groups)					MrsMattie	·		Re: Youngest person t...	24/11/97 17.
uk.consultants		58	58		Martin & Alethe...	·		Re: Information source...	24/11/97 18.
uk.current-events.general		45	45		JOANNE & JOS...	·		Games for language de...	24/11/97 21.
uk.d-i-y		236	236		Saad Medleg	·		test	Tue 03:11
⊟ uk.education.* (8 groups)					Phantom@strat...	·		Radar/Laser Scrambler...	Tue 07:45
uk.education.16plus		21	21		BBC Broadcast ...	·		BBC Online - a wealth ...	Tue 20:05
uk.education.expeditions		11	11		tekken@hotmail...	·		look here!!!!	Thu 07:19
uk.educatio...e-education		8	8		aeilkema@hotm...	·		JABA-software info	Fri 21:33
uk.education.maths		18	18						
uk.education.misc		35	35						
uk.education.schools-it		95	95						
uk.education.staffroom		30	30						
uk.education.teachers		54	54						
uk.environment		131	131						
uk.environme...conservation		28	28						
uk.finance		195	195						

Figure 4.4   Educational UseNet groups.

Once you've read the appropriate FAQ, you select which newsgroups you want to receive and can then both read postings to those newsgroups and reply to them using the same news server.

Every so often, the server that holds your postings will contact another server that carries UseNet and they each exchange new messages for that day. This type of daily exchange between computers that handle UseNet is repeated around the world, likening UseNet to a global distributed bulletin-board.

When using UseNet, you need to remember that because new messages are being sent from computer to computer across the globe, two people at different locations in the world might be viewing the same newsgroup at the same time, with each seeing slightly different content. Newer material will appear first on machines nearest to the server where it originated, gradually spreading out across the network.

Depending on the newsgroup, old messages might be kept for a few days or maybe for a month or so, but rarely longer. The amount of traffic generated across the 5000 or so newsgroups is such that there is rarely enough disk space on servers to keep messages for much longer. It is for this reason that many UseNet providers do not carry all the newsgroups.

Where education is concerned, this might not be a bad thing since there are some newsgroups that would be totally unsuitable for pupils. If you find that your Internet Provider offers a UseNet service, it might be worth asking if they could arrange for certain 'undesirable' newsgroups to be filtered out and not made available to your school.

On a positive note, there are several newsgroups that are of educational value. These carry not only messages of interest to teachers and pupils but files, which are not solely text, but can be graphics, software or sound. As with email, you may have to learn about encoding and compression formats (see 'Squeezing it all in', page 76) to view them.

Moreover, the same restrictions on large documents apply to newsgroups as to email. In order to post a large file to a newsgroup, such as a picture, the file often has to be split into several parts and these parts all encoded (using mostly UUEncode). The parts are then labelled in such a way ('part 2 of 3' etc) as to enable recipients to put them back together again in the right order, and once recombined, the file can be decoded using UUDecode or a similar package.

If all that sounds complicated, don't panic! There are several utilities or even *newsreaders* available that will automatically paste together the many parts of a UUEncoded file for you so it can be decoded. In addition, some modern newsreaders can display certain types of images without the need for compression or encoding.

Finally, if you are short of time but would like to view the most recent discussions about a particular topic, just use a *search engine* that searches UseNet postings. One particularly good search engine that only deals with newsgroups can be found on the Web at:

```
http://www.dejanews.com
```

Internet relay chat (IRC)

Until the emergence of the Web, communication on the Internet was conducted predominantly via a text interface. And despite the use of multimedia to smarten up Web pages, one of the most popular uses of the Internet remains email.

IRC is a form of online, real-time discussion using text as the main form of communication. Once you have the right piece of IRC software on your machine, you can link up with other individuals who have the software running by directing your software toward an IRC server (machine). It's a cross between a bulletin board and email.

Topics and themes are referred to as Channels. When you join a discussion on a theme or topic, you adopt an identity that you want to use during the chat. This identity could be based on true characteristics about yourself, or on a fictitious character. Then, any contributions you make to the chat appear on the screen alongside the comments of other contributors who are logged on to the chat channel at the same time.

At the start, IRC forums might appear somewhat confusing, with different comments appearing next to one another in no particular order, but you soon get used to the style. IRC is definitely not for novices so read the help file first before diving in. Like with everything, practice is the key.

IRC still tends to be dominated by trivial topics and undesirable subjects of discussion but there are the occasional educational gems out there, mainly based in the USA. On the whole, unless you can guarantee supervision, steer clear of using IRC with pupils until you are confident with the technology.

OTHER INTERNET TOOLS OF THE TRADE

File transfer protocol (FTP)

FTP has been around about as long as the Internet itself. FTP enables you to log-on to a computer and copy files from and to that computer using something called the file transfer protocol, hence the name FTP. To use FTP, it helps if you have the appropriate software on both the computers sending the file and the one receiving it. This *dedicated FTP software* is designed to make the whole process of sending and receiving files easier (Figure 4.5).

However, some Web browsers such as Netscape, Microsoft Internet Explorer, and Fresco let you access FTP servers in the same way you access World Wide Web servers and allow you to receive and send files. In fact, Web browsers make it so easy, you may have already used one to download a file from an FTP site without even knowing it. The only way to find out if you're connected to an FTP site using a Web browser is to look at the address at the top (the URL). If it's got the word 'ftp' in front of it, you know you've hit the jackpot.

Example:

ftp://ftp.demon.co.uk

However, you may find that dedicated FTP packages are often quicker at fetching and placing files via FTP than using a Web browser. If you think you'll be doing a great deal of file transfer, it would make sense to get yourself a dedicated package.

There are a number of dedicated FTP packages available. One example for each type of machine most commonly found in UK schools is given in 'Resources' on page 79. Search the Web for other examples by using one of the search tools mentioned in Part 1, Chapter 2.

One further crucial comment on FTP is required. When you access an FTP site you might find that the directory contains a list of folders and files. These will be listed by name, but you will not always have any other explanation as to what the folders might contain or what the files might be, whether they are pictures, or sounds or movies! If

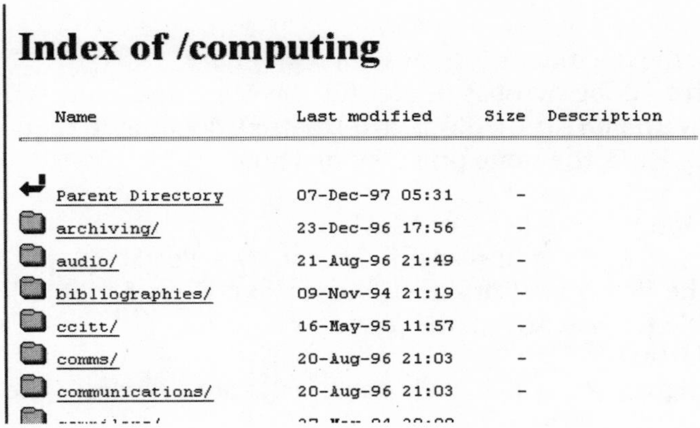

Index of /computing

Name	Last modified	Size	Description
↵ Parent Directory	07-Dec-97 05:31	-	
📁 archiving/	23-Dec-96 17:56	-	
📁 audio/	21-Aug-96 21:49	-	
📁 bibliographies/	09-Nov-94 21:19	-	
📁 ccitt/	16-May-95 11:57	-	
📁 comms/	20-Aug-96 21:03	-	
📁 communications/	20-Aug-96 21:03	-	

Figure 4.5 An FTP site viewed via a Web browser.

you're lucky, you might find a document called 'index' or 'readme' which gives you an index of the files on the site, but even these might not prove very helpful. At the moment, there's no foolproof way round this problem.

On your travels along the Internet route, you will find that many Internet sites make files available for a number of different computers: the IBM-compatible PC, Macintosh, Acorn, Unix, etc. Your browser can display some but not all of these formats, so you will probably need to be able to identify file types in order to know whether they will work on your computer. File types also reveal whether you will need additional software to decompress, play or view them.

The way you can identify the format of a file is by looking at its extension, which is usually expressed as a dot followed by two to four letters, the most common being three letters.

Typical file formats

.txt
A plain (ASCII) text file. File type: ASCII
Requires a word processor or a simple text editor to view them.
.doc
A formatted text file. File Type: ASCII
Files with this extension are not text documents but are often created using packages like Microsoft Word or WordPerfect for Windows.

73

.pdf
A portable document format file type: binary
Requires Adobe Acrobat Reader for the Macintosh and Windows to view them. A pdf file is a formatted document that, when viewed, looks the same on every machine.
.ps
A PostScript file. File type: ASCII
A PostScript file is unreadable except by a PostScript printer or with the help of an onscreen viewer like GhostScript, which is available for Macintosh and Windows.
.html/.htm
The language in which Web documents are authored. File type: ASCII
Requires a Web browser to view them.

At the moment, the graphics formats found on the Web are mainly those with the extension .GIF and .JPEG/.JPG. The great thing about these two formats is that they are platform-independent, which means you can use them on a PC, Macintosh or Acorn. Most modern Web Browsers can view these images. However, you might still come across other image formats, such as .tiff files, in which case you will need external viewers to view the image.

For video, the popular extensions are .AVI for the PC, .MPG (MPEG), which is platform-independent but requires its own player, and .MOV and .QT (QuickTime movies) which were initially for the Macintosh, but are now available for Windows.

The most popular extensions on the Web for sound are .WAV for the PC, .AIFF and .AU for the Macintosh. There is also .RA for Real Audio (see Part 1, Chapter 1) – a new system for delivering and playing real-time audio, that is, you can hear the sounds as soon as they start downloading to your machine rather than having to wait until the entire file is downloaded. The most common graphics, video and sound file formats are shown below.

Common file formats for graphics, video and sound

Graphics formats
If your Web browser cannot view GIFs or JPEGs, then you can use Lview Pro for Windows to view both types. For the Macintosh, you can use GIF Converter to view GIFs, and JPEGView to view JPEGs. ImageFS is available for the Acorn.

Video formats
.QT requires QuickTime, Sparkle or MoviePlayer on the Mac, and

QuickTime for Windows for the PC. .MOV files require Sparkle or MoviePlayer on the Mac, and QuickTime for Windows for the PC. .AVI requires AVI Video for Windows, and finally, .MPG files require Sparkle on the Macintosh and an MPEG Player for Windows. MovieFS is available for the Acorn.

Sound formats
Macintosh computers need Sound App to play .AU and .AIFF files; PCs can use WHAM (Waveform Hold and Modify). .RA files require a Real Audio Player, either for the Macintosh or Windows. Acorn machines could use SoundCon.

All graphics files can be viewed, created or manipulated with one of the commercially available graphics software programs like Photoshop for Windows or the Macintosh.

Finally, all the file formats found on the Internet can be broken into one of two basic types: ASCII format and BINARY format. ASCII files are text files you can view using any text editor or word processor, whereas binary files contain non-ASCII characters.

If you display a binary file on your screen, you will see a lot of strange symbols and characters that look like utter rubbish. In most cases, if you are not using a Web browser to download the file, you need to set your FTP software to the 'binary' setting to download sounds, images, movies or software. Some up-to-date FTP software can be placed on an 'automatic' setting that will automatically recognize whether the file is ASCII or BINARY.

Anonymous FTP
FTP files can be of any type: text, graphics, audio, video or even software. Most organizations, particularly educational ones, provide an enormous number of files free of charge to the public. All you pay for is the Internet connection and cost of the telephone call.

In order to gain access to this collection of files, you have to use your dedicated FTP software *or* your Web browser to log-on to the computer which has the files stored on it, that is, the FTP site. Organizations often require you to have a Username, an ID (identification) and a password to gain access to their FTP site but once you have access, you will be able to receive *and* place files at the site.

Luckily, if all you want to do is transfer files one-way, from the FTP site to your machine, there are many organizations that will let you log-on to the public part of their FTP site as an 'anonymous' user (see Figure 4.6). Basically, you type in your Username as 'anonymous'. You will be then be prompted for a password. It is customary on the Internet for 'anonymous' users to enter their email address as their password. After you have been given permission to log-on to the remote computer, you can transfer any file you find on the site to your own computer. It's a bit like logging-on to a local computer network and downloading files off the server.

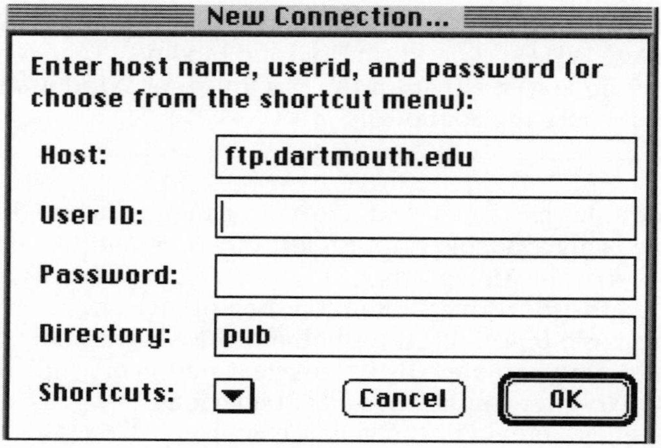

Figure 4.6   FTP software — typical opening screen.

As far as FTP is concerned, Web browsers are easier to use as they automatically log you into the FTP site as an 'anonymous' user and enter your email address as the password. In a Web browser, an FTP directory is presented as a list of links (Figure 4.7). Clicking on a directory link displays a subdirectory with its directories and files.

If, on the other hand, you have permission to log-on and place files on a site, you can use your FTP software or Web browser to also 'upload' (send) files to the site. FTP is still the method most commonly used to transfer ready-finished Web pages to a server (computer) in order for them to be viewed by anyone who has access to that server. Therefore, the ability to FTP files is an important skill to learn if you hope to set up a school Web site on a server that is *not* located in the school itself.

SQUEEZING IT ALL IN

If you intend to make extensive use of the resources you find on the Internet, you're going to have to learn about encoding and compression formats. As mentioned in the section on 'Electronic Mail' (see page 60), when files are sent via email they are encoded. If your email package does not deal with all the encoding formats, you will need separate

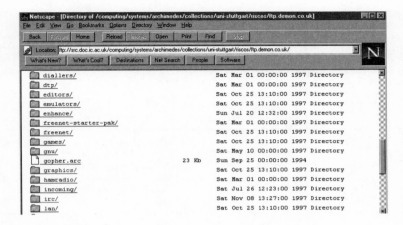

Figure 4.7 Directories on an FTP site.

software that can decode these files depending on which format was used to encode them in the first place.

But decoding the file is not always the end of the story. Files sent via email, and those available on UseNet newsgroups, FTP sites, and bulletin-boards, are very likely to be compressed too so as to take up less space on the server's hard disk.

Most of the files you encounter on the Web will either be text, graphics, audio or video files. Some may be compressed, others will not. The most common compressed files you will encounter are those with extensions like .ZIP, .HQX, or .ARC. These extensions represent the most commonly used compression formats for the PC, Macintosh and Acorn. Sometimes, you may encounter files with multiple extensions which usually means more than one type of software was used to compile and compress the file.

Example:

louvre.*zip* (the PKZIP format used by PCs)

Sites that deal with Acorn/Archimedes software compress using software called !Spark". !SparkPlug is available in the public domain to decompress these files. IBM-compatible machines use predominantly PKZip, while Macintosh machines use Binhex. But you're likely to come across a few other compression formats (tar, gzip) which are Unix-based since many servers that form part of the Internet are Unix machines.

Figure 4.8 summarizes the main compression and encoding formats and examples of the relevant software you will need to decompress them, depending on whether you're using an IBM, Macintosh or Acorn machine.

Extension	IBM-compatible	Macintosh	Acorn/ Archimedes
.zip Zip is the standard on MS-DOS machines...	For MSDOS: PKZip or PKUNZIP For Windows: WinZip or Stuffit Expander for Windows	Zip-IT (Shareware) PMPUnZip	!SparkFS
.arc	For Windows: Stuffit Expander for Windows.	Stuffit Expander (works in conjunction with the program StuffIt Lite, DropStuff with Expander Enhancer, or Stuffit Deluxe).	!SparkPlug
.sit (most common Mac archiving and compression program)	Stuffit Expander for Windows	Stuffit Lite 3.5 (shareware) Stuffit Expander for the Mac (extracts StuffIt archives but does not create them – freeware)	
.bin	Stuffit Expander for Windows	Stuffit Expander for the Mac (extracts StuffIt archives but does not create them – freeware)	
.gz, .z or .Z (gZip and Unix compress)	For MSDOS: gZip For Windows: Stuffit Expander for Windows.	MacGZip	
.hqx (BinHex – used to transmit data over text-based systems such as email enclosure files and net news)	PC BinHex (creates and extracts BinHex files) For Windows: Stuffit Expander for Windows	Compact Pro (can create and extract BinHex files – Shareware) Stuffit Expander for the Mac (decodes BinHex but can't encode it)	
MIME (Multipurpose Internet Mail Extensions) used to send data over email or net news	For MSDOS: MPack	MPack	Ant Ltd's Marcel
.uu and .uue (UUEncode) – used to enable transmission of data over email or UseNet news)	For MSDOS: uuCode UUDecode For Windows: Stuffit Expander for Windows	UULite (shareware) UUCD (freeware)	!SparkFS

Figure 4.8 Compression/decompression tools.

MAKING IT HAPPEN

There's only one way to find, install and use the tools mentioned in this section. You have to go on to the Internet and just do it. Some basic Internet tools are available on CD-ROMs sold with Internet magazines found in your local newsagent. They really can provide a cost-effective alternative to scouring the Net for tools.

RESOURCES

There are many browsers, email, Newsreaders and FTP packages available, most of them via the Internet itself. Many of the packages mentioned here are either shareware (you pay a nominal fee), freeware (they cost nothing) or commercial products.

Browsers

Netscape for Macintosh and PC:
http://home.netscape.com/comprod/upgrades/index.html
Internet Explorer for PC and Macintosh:
http://www.microsoft.com/microsoft.htm
ArcWeb for Acorn:
ftp.demon.co.uk/pub/archimedes/
Webster for Acorn:
ftp.demon.co.uk/pub/archimedes/developers

Email

Eudora for Macintosh:
ftp.eudora.com
Pegasus for PC:
ftp.risc.ua.edu/pub/network
Newsbase for Acorn:
ftp.src.doc.ic.ac.uk/computing/systems/archimedes/
collections/uni-stuttgart/riscos/comm/internet/mail/

FTP

Fetch for the Macintosh:
http://sunsite.doc.ic.ac.uk/packages/info-mac/comm/inet/
http://www.dartmouth.edu/pages/softdev/fetch.html

Using the Internet in Secondary Schools

FTP Explorer (Wind95):
http://ftpx.com/
WS_FTP (Windows 3.1):
http://www.ipswich.com/
SFTP for Acorn:
ftp.src.doc.ic.ac.uk/computing/systems/archimedes/
collections/uni-stuttgart/riscos/comm/internet/ftp/

Newsreaders (for UseNet)

Netreader for the Acorn:
ftp.src.doc.ic.ac.uk/computing/systems/archimedes/
collections/uni-stuttgart/riscos/ftp.demon.co.uk/
developers/
NewsWatcher for the Macintosh:
http://sunsite.doc.ic.ac.uk/packages/info-mac/comm/
_Internet/
Gravity (Win95):
http://www.anawave.com/
Free Agent (Windows 3.1):
http://www.forteinc.com/

Conferencing tools

CUSeeMe (Win95):
ftp.cu-seeme.cornell.edu/pub/video/win32/cuseeme.zip
CuSeeMe for Macintosh:
ftp.CU-SeeMe.cornell.edu/pub/CU-SeeMe/
Dwyco Video Conferencing System (PC):
http://www.dwyco.com/download/dwyco095.exe
FirstClass for Windows and Macintosh:
ftp.softarc.com/fc/clients/
NetMeeting (Win95):
http://www.microsoft.com/netmeeting/

Internet relay chat (IRC)

IRC for Acorn:
ftp.src.doc.ic.ac.uk/computing/systems/archimedes
/collections/uni-stuttgart/riscos/ftp.demon.co.uk/irc/
mIRC (Win95 and Windows 3.1):
http://ww.mirc.co.uk/
M_ircle for the Macintosh:
http://www.xs4all.nl/~ii/

80

Compression and decompression tools

Sparkplug for the Acorn:
ftp.demon.co.uk/pub/archimedes/
http://www.netlink.co.uk/users/pilling/
SparkFS for the Acorn: Available direct from David Pilling; email
david@pilling.demon.co.uk
http://www.netlink.co.uk/users/pilling/
Stuffit Expander for Windows and Macintosh:
ftp.aladdinsys.com
PKZip (Win 95 and Windows 3.1):
ftp.simtel.net
WinZip (for Win95 and Windows 3.1):
ftp.oak.oakland.edu
Uuencode/Uudecode for PC:
ftp.mirrors.aol.com
MacGZip, Binhex, mpac, UUCD, Zip-IT, UULite all for the Macintosh:
ftp.src.doc.ic.ac.uk/computing/systems/mac/Collections
/sumex/comm/util/_compress_%26_Translate/

Sounds

SoundCon for Acorn:
ftp.src.doc.ic.ac.uk/computing/systems/archimedes/uni-
stuttgart/riscos/comm/internt/ftp/
PlayAVI for the Acorn:
ftp.demon.co.uk/pub/mirros/hensa/micros/arch/riscos/b/
WHAM (Waveform Hold and Modify) (Windows 3.1):
http://www.winsite.com/info/pc/win3/sounds/wham133.zip
Sound App for the Macintosh:
ftp.src.doc.ic.ac.uk/computing/systems/mac/Collections
/sumex/_Graphic_526_Sound_Tool/_Movie/
Authorware Professional for Windows (AVI Player):
ftp.umbc.net
Real Audio (Win95) and for the Macintosh:
http://www.realaudio.com/

Graphics

ImageFS for the Acorn:
Alternative Publishing Ltd, 30 Clyde Place, Glasgow G5 8AG
FYEO (For Your Eyes Only) GIF and JPEG Viewer for Acorn:
ftp.src.doc.ic.ac.uk/computing/systems/archimedes

```
/collections/uni-stuttgart/riscos/ftp.demon.co.uk/
graphics/
```
JPEGView for Macintosh:
GIF Converter for Macintosh:
```
ftp.src.doc.ic.ac.uk/computing/systems/mac/Collections
/sumex/_Graphic_526_Sound_Tool/_Movie/
```
Lview Pro (Win95):
```
ftp.src.doc.ic.ac.uk/computing/systems/ibmpc/
collections/simtel/win95/graphics/
```

Video

MovieFS for Acorn (commercial package):
```
http://www.wss.co.uk/
```
Sparkle for the Macintosh:
```
ftp.src.doc.ic.ac.uk/computing/systems/mac/Collections/
sumex/_Graphic_526_Sound_Tool/_Sound/
```
Quicktime for Macintosh and Windows:
```
ftp.quicktime.apple com
```
MoviePlayer for Macintosh:
```
ftp1.info.apple.com
```
ADI MPEG Player (Win95):
```
http://www.adi.net
```

Integrated packages for the Acorn

Overall, you will find more software available for the PC and Macintosh than for the Acorn. However, for a full and integrated approach to your Internet needs on an Acorn machine, try DoggySoft Ltd or Ant Ltd.

Doggysoft produce Termite – a complete Internet solution for the Acorn machine. It includes a World Wide Web browser with which you can also use FTP. Termite provides both an on- and offline email package:
Doggysoft Ltd, Furzefield House, Furzefield Road, Beaconsfield, Bucks. HP9 1PQ,UK. Telephone (01494) 673222; Fax (01494) 675878 or email sales@doggysoft.co.uk or support@doggysoft.co.uk. or
dial Furzefield Hq, their support Bulletin-Board on (01494) 681711;

Internet Suite Release II by Ant Ltd offer Marcel for email, Fresco as the offline email and newsreader and an FTP package. Ant Ltd, PO Box 300, Cambridge, CB1 2EG. Telephone (01223) 567808. Fax (01223) 567801. Email sales/enquiries (sales@ant.co.uk). Web: http://www.ant.co.uk.

Part 2

Part 2

Chapter 5

Curriculum activities

INTRODUCTION

In this section of the book the focus is on using the Internet in the curriculum. It is organized into the curriculum areas of Science (Physics, Chemistry, Biology), Mathematics, English, Geography, History, Design and Technology, Music, Art, Modern Languages and Religious Education. Each of these areas of study is presented with an introduction and a number of related activities. In most cases the activities consist of teacher notes and pupil activity sheets. For Science, Mathematics, English and Design and Technology, the activities are at Key Stage 3 and 4; for the remaining areas the activities are at Key Stage 3.

The activities try to use the full potential of the Internet. They are challenging and aim to help pupils become critical and largely autonomous users of information technology (IT). Most of the activities involve pupils in accessing the Web and using appropriate search tools. Some activities require pupils to have Web page construction skills. Since these skills do not require computer programming skills (see Part 1, Chapter 3), they are readily accessible for pupils at Key Stage 3.

In some activities pupils are asked to download files from the Internet. In many cases this is a straightforward activity but it does require knowledge on how to store files on the computer's hard disk (see Part 1, Chapter 1). A number of the activities make use of the multimedia facilities of the Web. A computer with a sound card is therefore an essential requirement.

The communication ability of the Internet is utilized in some of the activities. Pupils are invited to send emails and participate in online conferencing (see Part 1, Chapter 2). The Internet, particularly the Web, can facilitate and support collaborative working (see Part 1, Chapter 4) and this is an approach which is chosen in several of the activities by adopting group roles or by using electronic communication technologies.

There is no time allotted to the activities. The majority of them can be adapted to fit within a double class period or spread, in project fashion, over a longer length of time. Some activities do require some form of preparation by the pupils and where this is necessary, it has been highlighted in the teacher notes.

It is hoped that you will not just read the activities associated with your curriculum area. The Internet provides support for a number of different valuable teaching approaches. We have tried to incorporate what we think is appropriate in your curriculum area but some of the other subject areas might provide ideas for further fruitful development. So please browse other activities.

SCIENCE

Introduction

The strands of the UK IT National Curriculum that are particularly relevant to Science and the Web are:

- communicating information that involves modifying and presenting information in a variety of ways incorporating words, pictures, numbers and sound
- handling information that involves storing, retrieving and presenting factual information
- modelling which involves using simulations of real or imaginary events to identify changes and trends.

The use of the Internet and particularly the Web in Science has opened up new opportunities for the science educator to link the requirements of IT capability with the science curriculum. The Internet will not replace the investigation and cannot as yet replace traditional data-logging and modelling software. One can however see a future where this might be possible. The Bradford Robotic Telescope at:

http://www.telescope.org/

allows teachers and pupils to control it from a distance and there are sites in the USA where it is possible to observe online dissections and get involved with some very interesting examples of scientific models. For an entertaining example of scientific modelling (mostly 'A' level) visit:

http://www.Colorado.EDU/physics/2000/applets
/index.html

It is hoped that the activities described in the following pages can contribute to development in this area. Some of them use the Web as information sources but in other activities (Acid Rain) pupils are encouraged to submit information to a National Database and then to use this database for theory-constructing and testing.

The activities in the following pages try to involve as much Sc1 as possible. They are challenging with respect to both IT and science skills.

Activity Science 1 – the circulatory system

Teacher notes

National Curriculum	Key Stage 3 Life Processes and Living Things: 2f
Activity aims	To introduce the role of heart as part of the circulatory system of our bodies. To use the Web as a multimedia information source

The Franklin Institute has a very good site that is devoted to the human heart and the body's circulatory system. The pupils should spend time on these pages reinforcing their knowledge of the three main parts of the circulatory system.

http://www.fi.edu/biosci/

They will then be able to go to Blood Vessels and explore the way in which these work. There is a video on travelling through arteries, which may be found during this exploration. The video is in .MOV format so an appropriate player will need to be downloaded (see Part 1, Chapter 4).

After examining the functioning of the heart the pupils can pretend they are listening to heartbeats through a stethoscope on:

The Franklin Institute
http://www.fi.edu/biosci/monitor/heartbeat.html

If you cannot play this video you can get the appropriate software from:
http://tucows.rmplc.co.uk/

a site which has all the necessary downloading facilities.

The pupils can check their own health factors by measuring their pulse rate. This is explained on one of the activity pages of the site and includes a short video sequence that shows the pulse points on the body.

There is no pupils' activity sheet with this activity.

Activity Science 2 – foxes and rabbits – food chains, webs and pyramids

Teacher notes

National Curriculum	Key Stage 3 Life Processes and Living Things: 5c, 5d, 5f, 5g Experimental and Investigative Science: 3a, 3b, 3d, 3f
Activity aims	To offer the opportunity of interacting with a dynamic three-layer food chain. To practise downloading files to the hard or floppy disk

At the time of press the software outlined on this page was only available for PC-compatible computers.

This page examines a system of three trophic levels by investigating the relationship between grass, rabbits and foxes. Pupils will need an understanding of food pyramids and the struggle to balance appropriate biomass with the herbivores and carnivores.

Pupils need to download a program from the Web and to store it in an appropriate place on the hard disk of the computer. A trial version of the program is available at:

Creatures site
http://www.fssc.demon.co.uk/Creatures/creature.htm

Procedures for doing this are outlined in Part 1, Chapter 1 of this book.

The program will need to be run from the File Manager (Win 3.1) or Explorer (Win 95) and as it is a special edition it will only run for 120 seconds. To rerun it needs reloading by clicking on the *Creature.exe* icon. The whole process can be made easier in Windows 95 by creating a short-cut and placing the *Creatures* icon on the opening screen (Figure 5.1).

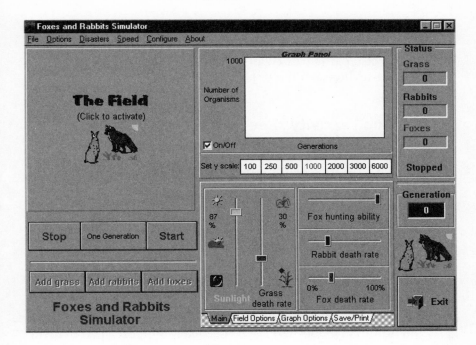

Figure 5.1 The creatures program.

With knowledge of the basics of a food pyramid the pupils should soon be able to handle the number of foxes, rabbits and amount of grass to create a successfully sustainable environment.

The action takes place in a 'Field', which at the start of the program is covered. An area in the top left-hand side of the screen has to be clicked on to show the 'The Field' in which the action takes place. Once the field appears grass, rabbits and foxes can be added.

It might be worth buying a copy of the program so that pupils could use it in a more sophisticated way at a later stage. The program is available from:

Future Skills Software
Penroydn
Pontrhydygroes
Ystrad Meurig
Dyfed, SY25 6DP

Pupils can get some preliminary support material from:

Science Education Associations Server
http://science.cc.uwf.edu/sh/curr/foodchain/
foodchain.htm

where they can get access to a glossary of terms associated with food-chains.

Pupils can also participate in an online quiz and test their score. The questions are included in the pupil activity sheet.

Pupil activity sheet – foxes and rabbits

This exercise asks you to examine a food-chain and try to estimate the survival characteristics of the different trophic levels and the food pyramid.

Look first at a site that gives you some information on this food-chain and a useful glossary of terms associated with this area of study.

```
http://science.cc.uwf.edu/sh/curr/foodchain/
foodchain.htm
```

It might be useful to print out these pages.

Find out as much information as you can about a food pyramid which starts with sunlight and grass, and ends with foxes. Estimate how much grass and how many rabbits might be needed to support a pair of foxes, then go to:

```
http://www.fssc.demon.co.uk/Creatures/creature.htm
```

where you can download the *Creatures* program. This is achieved by following the screen instructions and saving the program to the hard disk in an appropriate file or folder. When the download has finished, go to the File Manager or Windows Explorer, find the downloaded program, click on it and you will get a black screen which shows that the program has been loaded in the file.

Click on the 'Creature.exe' file that starts the program. You now have only 120 seconds to supply the potential data and see what happens. When the 120 seconds is up click on the *terminate* button and start again. Can you create a sustainable environment?

Look at the graph that is generated on the screen. This is a record of the events so try to interpret from the graph how you will change your next attempt at creating a sustainable environment.

You can complete your work and research on food chains and pyramids by thinking about the questions shown below in the 'ecology quiz'. The possible answers are in the brackets. You can then check on your answers by going to:

The York Region Board of Education
```
http://www.yrbe.edu.on.ca/~mdhs/compsci/dpt3ar/ecology/
ecoquiz.htm
```

The ecology quiz

1. Which of the following is not the same as the others? *(herbivore, second order consumer, cow, first order consumer)*
2. Which kind of interaction between organisms is not a form of symbiosis? *(parasitism, commensalism, mutalism, competition)*
3. Which of the following is not an example of a biome? *(tundra, grasslands, desert, tropical rainforest)*
4. Which of the following is an abiotic factor? *(seaweed, fish, sun's radiation, rabbit)*
5. Which of the following is a valid food chain? *(grass->rabbit->wolf, rabbit-> grass->wolf, wolf->grass-.rabbit, grass-.wolf-.rabbit)*
6. Which of the following characteristics does not apply to grasslands? *(greatest diversity of organisms, fertile soil, tall grass)*
7. Which is one of the ways that predators use to overcome their prey? *(being friends with the prey, surprise attack on the prey, bribing the prey, giving the prey a box of chocolates)*
8. Which of the following is not one of the types of food pyramids? *(biomass, energy, number, volume)*
9. Which of the following is not one of the types of soil? *(graphite, loam, sand, humus)*
10. Which is not a way that an animal can become endangered? *(loss of habitat, alien influence, loss of food source, disease)*

Activity Science 3 – the periodic table

Teacher notes

National Curriculum	Key Stage 4 Experimental and Investigative Science: 3a, 3c, 3d Materials and their Properties: 1d, 3a, 3b, 3c
Activity aim	To generate ideas on relationship patterns using an interactive periodic table. To use the Web as an interactive information source

The periodic table is represented in many forms on the Internet but probably the best is to be found at:

The University of Sheffield
http://www.shef.ac.uk/~chem/web-elements/

'Web Elements' is the first and most comprehensive interactive periodic table on the Web. Using this resource, pupils can get a wealth of information about the elements and their reactions. It has a small audio element where a distant voice names the elements and it contains some of the following information that your pupils might be able to use.

General information

- key data and description
- historical
- uses

Chemical data compounds

- electronegativities
- bond enthalpies
- lattice energies
- radii
- reduction potentials

Crystallography

- crystal structure

Physical data

- bulk properties
- thermal properties
- thermodynamic properties

Isotopes

- naturally occurring isotopes
- radioactive isotopes

As is apparent from this data this site is useful for A-level students as well as Key Stage 4 (Figure 5.2).

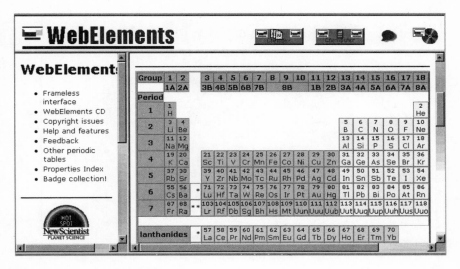

Figure 5.2 Web elements.

The activity sheet asks the pupils to use the periodic table to look for patterns and trends and create some graphs. Your use of it will depend on the time available. The activity sheet also refers pupils to a world map at:

Xerox.Parc.Map Viewer
http://pubweb.parc.xerox.com/map

The pupils will need to copy the map from the screen (Figure 5.3) and print it at an appropriate size.

Pupil activity sheet – the periodic table

There are about 45 common elements and almost 55 uncommon ones. It was found that groups of these elements had certain characteristics in common. For example, some were gases, which had great stability and very reluctantly reacted with any other element, while others were metals and were highly reactive. The organization of the elements into groups resulted in the periodic table.

The following Web page has a periodic table that contains all of the known elements and is highly interactive:

The University of Sheffield University
http://www.shef.ac.uk/~chem/web-elements/

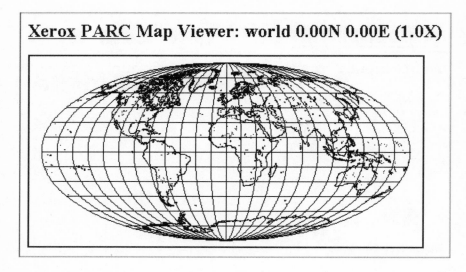

Figure 5.3 The Xerox.Parc.Map Viewer.

For the elements: aluminum, argon, arsenic, barium, bromine, calcium, carbon, chromium, cobalt, fluorine, gold, helium, hydrogen, iodine, iron, krypton, lead, lithium, magnesium, mercury, neon, nickel, nitrogen, oxygen, phosphorous, platinum, potassium, silicon, silver sodium, strontium, sulphur, tin, tungsten, xenon, zinc:

- plot on a world map the location of the discovery site of each element.

You could use the map that is on:

Xerox. Map Viewer
`http://pubweb.parc.xerox.com/map`

- Make a timeline to show the discovery date of each element.
- Trace the language history of the names of five of the elements.
- Write a biographical report on the discoverer of the most common element in the human body.
- Make a bar graph showing the value (£/gram) of each element.
- Identify the two elements *most* active and the two elements least active. Compare and contrast their properties.
- Identify the two elements that are used most often in industrial situations.
- Identify the two elements most useful in the medical field.
- Identify the element that would have the most economic impact if the natural reserves were consumed.

Activity Science 4 – acid rain

Teacher notes

National Curriculum	Key Stage 3 Experimental and Investigative Science: 1a, 1b, 1c, 1g, 2a, 2b, 2d, 3d Life Processes and Living Things: 5e Material and their Properties: 1h, 3e, 3f, 3h, 3i
Activity aims	To research acid rain and contribute to a national survey. To communicate using the Web

This activity will require resources that will enable pupils to collect rainwater and accurately measure pH. It is a magnificent opportunity to join a nationwide study of very important phenomena, which has the potential for causing severe ecological damage.

As rain falls it dissolves gases like oxygen and carbon dioxide and as carbon dioxide forms a weak acid in the water. The normal pH of the rain is about pH 5 or 6. (Neutral water will have a pH of 7 and acidity increases with decreasing pH.) If the atmosphere is polluted with nitrogen or sulphur oxides, the rain becomes more acidic and pH falls to 4 or lower.

Pupils can find information about the damage that acid rain can cause on:

The Quebec English Schools Network
http://www.qesn.meq.gouv.qc.ca/ssn/acidrain/handouts.htm
Queens University at Kingston, Ontario
http://qlink.queensu.ca/~4lrm4/table.htm

or search for acid rain resources on the Web. The activity sheet asks questions about acid rain that can be answered by referring to these resources.

Pupil activity sheet – acid rain

Acid rain can cause some serious problems to the environment and information on this is given on the following pages:

http://www.qesn.meq.gouv.qc.ca/ssn/acidrain/handouts.htm
http://qlink.queensu.ca/~4lrm4/table.htm

Use the information on these pages, or use a search engine, to answer the following questions:

1. What is acid rain?
2. Name three ways the fumes that cause acid rain are produced.
3. Put these three statements about how acid rain is formed in the right order:
   - Rain, snow and fog bring the acid solution back to the earth.
   - The fumes combine with the moisture in the air to form solutions of pH less than 7.
   - Burning fossil fuels produces sulphurous and nitric fumes.
4. Name the two most important chemicals that cause acid rain.
5. Explain why non-industrial areas are affected by acid rain.

You are now going to take part in a National Survey on acid rain in the UK. You will have to find out how to collect rain and accurately measure the pH of it. It is important that the experiment that you carry out is a fair one and that you have considered all the factors that could effect your result. We would like you to collect the following data about the rain in your area as often as you like over the next few years.

Date:
Precipitation

- Amount (ml)
- pH

Source of weather and direction from which it came.

You will then submit this information to the form on the acid rain page found at:

University of Central England
http://www.uce.ac.uk/education/cript/rain/htm

Your information will be placed on a map of the United Kingdom with those of other schools. Acid rain is also a natural phenomenon. A pH of 5.6 is the pH value of carbon dioxide in equilibrium with distilled water. Hence, acid ran is defined as any rainfall that has an acidity level beyond what is expected in non-polluted rainfall. Any precipitation that has a pH value of less than 5.6 is considered to be acid precipitation.

Activity Science 5 – making it easier

Teacher notes

National Curriculum	Key Stage 3 Experimental and Investigative Science: 1b, 1c, 1d, 3a, 3g, 4b, 4c Physical Processes: 2b, 2f Key Stage 4 Physical Processes: 5f (energy and power)
Activity aims	To investigate the role of pulleys in lifting loads. To use the Web as an information source

This activity will need to be supported with resources that will enable the pupils to use pulleys and measure the forces involved.

This uses the resources of the *The Society of Automotive Engineers* (SAE) and their Web site at:

Canada's school net
http://schoolnet2.carleton.ca/english/math_sci/phys/worldinmotion/

There are five units of work on this site which focus on moving and simple machines, ie slopes, pulleys and gears. There is an .AVI (see Part 1, Chapter 4) movie that can be viewed by the pupils but this is a little dated and is not really worth the download time. A useful way of working on this site is to download all the pages (total 1.5MB) using an offline browser (see Part 1, Chapter 1). *Teleport Pro* is an excellent offline browsing tool and can be found at:

http://www.tenmax.com

The pupil activity sheet focuses on Unit 4 that looks at pulleys. The resources are those which can be found in the home although you might decide to replace them with some from your own resources. The activity could be considered at the Key Stage 3/4 borderline. So to place it firmly into Key Stage 3 you may decide to focus on the forces involved rather than on the total work done.

Pupils will be expected to have access to pulley construction material and maybe Newton meters instead of the elastic bands used on the instruction sheets.

Equipment required:

- two brooms – these are for pulleys
- rope, 1 cm thick, 10 m long
- garden gloves – so the pupils' hands are not hurt when pulling on the pulley rope
- two medium-sized cotton reels – these are for the smaller pulleys with the two pencils acting as axles
- string, 50 cm – this is the small pulley string
- rubber band – this is to measure the pull and can be replaced by a Newton meter
- scissors
- 20 heavy washers – these will be part of the load when using the pulley. Alternatively you could use ordinary 10 g and 100 g masses
- several 3-oz paper cups – the carrier of the load
- some toothpicks – for making the carrying handle for the cup
- two pipe cleaners – for fixing the pencil axles to supports
- pushpin – to make holes in the paper cups
- metre rule
- two pencils – the axles.

It is suggested in the activity sheet that the pupils print the instruction and the pictures.

Pupil activity sheet – making it easier

Putting a large crate on to a lorry could be a difficult task. The crate could be lifted on, pushed up an inclined plane, or maybe a set of pulleys could help in the lift. Whatever way the crate reaches the back of the lorry the total energy transferred to the crate is the same. The inclined plane and the pulleys just make the job easier. The inclined plane and the pulleys are called machines. Machines are devices that enable us to do things more easily.

In this activity you are going to investigate some of these ideas. Does a pulley make things easier? How does a pulley system do this? Is the total amount of energy transferred the same?

The pages that you will use are at:
`http://schoolnet2.carleton.ca/english/math_sci/phys/worldinmotion/`

Go to this page and then click on Unit 4 and go to the section labelled 'Pull down to go up'.

Print the pages and carry out the activity. Instead of using an elastic band to measure the pull you can use a Newton meter and instead of washers you might be able to use 10 g and 100 g masses. When you have finished the activity try the investigation and see whether twice the load means twice the effort.

Now move on to the next section *Pulling together* and continue your investigation of pulleys.

Report on how much force and how much energy is needed to raise the load when you are using one pulley and two pulleys.

Activity Science 6 – the story of a planet

Teacher notes

National Curriculum	Key Stage 3
	Physical Processes: 4a, 4b, 4c, 4d, 4e
Activity aims	To collate data about the planets. To use
	the Web as a publication medium

This activity uses the vast resources of the Web, which are focused on the Earth and Space. Prominent among these sites is the NASA site at:

The Jet Propulsion Laboratory, NASA
http://www.jpl.nasa.gov/

This is a remarkable site with links to most of the space exploration projects. If you want the latest information on ongoing exploration go to the Press release section on the opening page.

Another excellent site is the Nine Planets site at:

Students for the Exploration and Development of Space. The Nine Planets
http://seds.lpl.arizona.edu/nineplanets/nineplanets/
nineplanets.html

This site will give you all the statistical data that you will need for the completion of the activity.

If you want to develop the work on 'The Earth and Beyond' into further curriculum areas then visit the Centre for Alternative Energy site and download the quiz. Pupils can be asked to use the Web to find the answers and then you can direct them to the CAT site to check their answers. The CAT site is:

Centre for Alternative Technology
http://Web2.cat.org.uk/cat/

The activity asks pupils to create a multimedia Web page for one planet using information they can get from Web pages or from other sources. The advantage of Web sources is that pictures can easily be saved to disk and then cut and pasted into their document. The CD-ROM *Encarta* and other sources can also be used, but pupils should be encouraged to visit the NASA pages and get photographs of planets and moons that have only recently been surveyed by different probes.

You will need to prepare the basic Web pages using a Web authoring package such as Microsoft *FrontPage* or an equivalent authoring tool (see Part 1, Chapter 3) and have available a graphics package such as *Paint Shop Pro*.

Pupil activity sheet – the story of a planet

In this activity your group is asked to produce a presentation on a planet of our solar system. The teacher will allocate the planet to you. The presentation will be in the format of a Web document that will contain at least ten linked pages (Figure 5.4).

Figure 5.4   The story of a planet.

When working as a group you may find that if you assign individuals to particular tasks you will be more productive. If you decide to work in this way some of the roles you might adopt are:

Director   –   responsible for making sure that all those involved in the production are working towards the same objective.

Researcher   –   responsible for finding out information about the planet.

Story writer –   responsible for constructing the storyboard, requesting information and overseeing production.

Producer   –   responsible for producing the story on the screen.

Before you start collecting information, the group will need to decide on the story. To do this you will need to have some information on your planet from books, CD-ROM or the Web. You can then decide upon the story. It could be something like 'A day in my life'.

This will then help you construct the storyboard that will provide you with the production plan. The researcher and producer can then start the construction with the rest helping. Pictures can be downloaded from the Web and from other resources into your Web document.

Try to make the presentation as interesting as possible. Think of the colour of the text, its size and the background (see Part 1, Chapter 3). Do not make the pictures too big and if you need to change them use software that is designed to help with Web page construction.

MATHEMATICS

Introduction

There are a large number of mathematics sites on the Web. An excellent reference site is found at:

Some Mathematics Education Sites on Web by Richard Phillips
`http://acorn.educ.nottingham.ac.uk/Maths/other/`

This page contains almost 60 links to other sites including another reference site at the National Council for Educational Technology:

Curriculum IT support for Mathematics
`http://vtc.ngfl.gov.uk/resource/cits/maths`

This site is the home of CITS (Curriculum IT Support for mathematics) and should be a bookmark for any mathematics teacher.

For the teacher of mathematics the Web provides many opportunities for the development of IT capability within a mathematical context.

The IT strands that are particularly relevant to mathematics and the Web are:

- handling information, which involves storing, retrieving and presenting factual information
- modelling, which can be used to study mathematical functions, eg through testing hypothesis
- communicating information, which involves modifying and presenting information in a variety of ways incorporating words, pictures, numbers and sound.

The activities below try to show how the Web can be used to develop mathematical skills linked to the IT capability. They cover most of the areas of the mathematics programmes of study and can be considered as examples of how to use the Web in those areas. The use of the Web in mathematics teaching is limited only by the limits of imagination of the curriculum planner.

Activity Maths 1 – decorating

Teacher notes

National Curriculum	Key Stage 3 Using and Applying Mathematics: 1a, 1b, 2a, 2c Number: 1a, 2a
Activity aims	To develop mathematical skills To use the Web in an interactive manner

This is an activity that can be used to introduce the idea of the Web as an information processing tool and to develop mathematical skills. You will need measuring equipment for this activity.

The activity uses a paint estimator program on the Dulux site. The pupils are asked to measure the classroom, or more challengingly the hall or stairwell and to estimate the amount of paint that is needed. Pupils will need to make allowances for the windows, doors and other features. They will also need to make judgements on the type of paint needed.

```
http://www.dulux.com/cgi-bin/retail/sel-enq.pl
```

is a site which will help.

After finding the area they can estimate the amount of paint needed using the data on the pupil sheet and then check this by using the calculator found at:

`http://www.dulux.com/cgi-bin/retail/calc.pl`

An alternative to the measurement exercise is to use the model room on the pupils' activity sheet.

Pupil activity sheet – decorating

This activity uses the *ICI Dulux* pages to help you choose paint to decorate your classroom or house. If you decide that it is the classroom, hall or stairwell of your school which needs painting, then you will need to measure it.

Ensure that you make allowances for windows and doors in your calculations. After you have found the area of surface that needs painting, you will have to decide on the type of paint required.

You can go to:

`http://www.dulux.com/cgi-bin/retail/sel-enq.pl`

to help you decide on this. This site gives you a great deal of information on the properties of the different paints. For some of the more common paints, the area of surface that they cover is given in the example below:

> Vinyl Matt 13 sq. metres per litre
> Vinyl Silk 13 sq. metres per litre
> Solid Emulsion 12 sq. metres per litre
> Non Drip gloss 11 sq. metres per litre
> Non Drip varnish 16 sq. metres per litre
> Once gloss 10 sq. metres per litre

Using this information you can calculate the amount of paint required for your surface and you can check this with the Dulux calculation on:

`http://www.dulux.com/cgi-bin/retail/calc.pl`

If they are not the same can you explain why?

Activity Maths 2 – saving and borrowing

Teacher notes

National Curriculum	Key Stage 4 Using and Applying Mathematics: 1a, 1b, 1c, 3a Number: 3c, 3d
Activity aims	To develop ideas on compound interest. The opportunity to use the Web as an information source

The Internet is now a major source of information about interest rates. Most of the major banks and building societies have sites on the Internet where you can find information, although this is more readily obtainable from the building societies than the banks.

Pupils are given an example and are asked to work out the best gross rate for an investment over a period of time and the same for a loan over the same period. Then pupils are asked to solve a problem in which £2000 is placed into an account of the Woolwich Building Society. Pupils are asked to calculate what the gross sum would be after three years. Go to:

http://www.woolwich.co.uk

for the latest interest rates. It is important for most pupils to reinforce the difference between the gross and the net sum.

After calculating the sums of money, pupils are asked to investigate the sites of other banks and building societies to find which offers the best rates for investment and borrowing. One particularly helpful site is the Halifax:

Halifax Society
http://www.halifax.co.uk

To get to the list of all banks and building societies that have pages on the Internet, ask pupils to use the Yahoo search tool (see Part 1, Chapter 2). If they type in the keyword 'banks' and then search in the UK only, they will arrive at a category 'United Kingdom Business: companies: Financial services: Banking: Banks' which will then take them to a list of banks. Alternatively, you could point them to some of the specialist search devices which are also listed in this section.

The Abbey National Web page has a calculator that allows borrowers to type in the amount of loan and then gives them the total payments based upon interest rates at the time. It could be a useful site to check some calculations.

Pupil activity sheet – saving and borrowing

If you save some money in a savings account with a bank or a building society it will earn interest because they will be using that money. Similarly if you borrow money from a bank or a building society you will have to pay them interest. The amount of interest depends on the amount you have borrowed or saved, the length of time that you leave the money in the bank or borrow it for and the interest rate.

For example: a friend places £100 in the ABC building society and they pay interest at 4 per cent per annum (each year). If the interest earned stays in the account, how much will your friend have in the account at the end of the fourth year?

Year	Amount saved
1	£100 × 1.04
2	£100 × 1.04 × 1.04 = £100 × $(1.04)^2$
3	
4	£100 × $(1.04)^4$ =

Most of the banks and building societies in the United Kingdom and the world have pages on the Internet. Some of the banks give their interest rates on these pages. Imagine you want to save £2000 for 4 years. Go to:

http://www.woolwich.co uk

Look for the savings/investment page and find the rate of interest for investing the money in a current account. Calculate how much the £2000 will be worth after four years. The interest you will use will be the gross interest rate.

Now look at the cost of borrowing £2000 for four years. Look at some other banks and building societies to find out which is the most competitive for lending and borrowing. To find the other banks and building societies use a subject directory such as:

http://www.yahoo.co.uk

Type 'banks' in the search box. Click on *search UK only*. This will bring up a category called 'United Kingdom Business: Companies: Financial Services :Banking: Banks'. Clicking on this will give all the banks and building societies in the UK with Internet pages.

Activity Maths 3 – special triangles

Teacher notes

National Curriculum	Key Stage 3 Using and Applying Mathematics: 1a, 1b, 1c, 3a, 4a Shape, Space and Measures: 2b, 2c, 2d
Activity aims	To arrive at a definition of similar triangles. To use an important Web mathematics site

This lesson uses a famous mathematics site:

The Maths Forum
http://forum.swarthmore.edu

This US site is a Mathematics Education Community Centre on the Internet. It is a major source of mathematical ideas and also the home of *Dr. Maths*, a service that answers pupils' mathematical questions.

The site that we will use for similar triangles is:

http://forum.swarthmore.edu/~sarah/shapiro/
sum.angles.html

This contains a worksheet that can be either printed or used online. On the worksheet there are three circles with triangles within them. Ask the pupils to find five triangles illustrated in Figure 5.5 that have the same shape but are different in size. The pupils can copy the triangles on to graph paper and turn them so that they all have the same orientation.

Using the screen print triangles, ask the pupils to determine the interior angles of the chosen triangles and label the angles on their copies.

The pupils can then do the same with the other two diagrams finding similar triangles inside them. They will find that there are not so many in this case. They can then decide for themselves what is special about similar triangles.

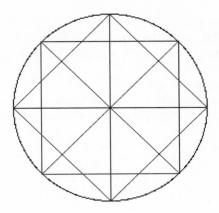

Figure 5.5 An example of five triangles.

Similar triangles are quite important in the art of origami, so after the definition of similar triangles is arrived at, it could be worth while looking at some origami patterns and see if it does play as important a part.

A site that might be useful here is the UK National Origami Society at:

UK National Origami Society
`http://nw.demon.co.uk/rpmrecords/bos/index.html`

Links from this page lead to a Web page by Nick Robinson where there are some designs of paper planes and other things to make.

There are a vast number of mathematical opportunities on the Swarthmore site that could lead to alternative Web-linked teaching opportunities.

Pupil activity sheet – special triangles

For this activity go to the following site:

`http://forum.swarthmore.edu/~sarah/shapiro/`
`sum.angles.html`

Print the page.

How many triangles can you find in the top diagram? Find five triangles in the top diagram that have the same shape but are different in size. You can do this by carefully copying the triangles on to graph paper and turning them so that they all have the same orientation.

Given that the sum of the angles of a triangle = 180° and the sum of the angles of the vertices at the centre of a circle = 360°, find the interior angles of the chosen triangles from the printed image. Label these interior angles on your copies.

Repeat this exercise for the second and third diagram. How many can you find and how many are the same shape? What is special about the triangles that you have found? Why do you think they are called similar triangles?

Similar triangles are very important in the art of origami (paper folding). Go to:

```
http://nw.demon.co.uk/rpmrecords/bos/index.html
```

Search the site and see if you can find which show similar triangles in the paper designs.

Activity Maths 4 – graph it

Teacher notes

National Curriculum	Key Stage 3 Using and Applying Mathematics: 1a Algebra: 2d, 3b
Activity aim	To develop graph skills using real situations. To access and use up-to-date data from the Web

If pupils would like to get some general information on different types of graph, then Bob Hoffmann has an excellent site at:

Encyclopedia of Educational Technology
```
http://edweb.sdsu.edu/edweb_folder/EET/Graphs/
Graphs.html
```

To generate a graph, two sets of data are needed. If both of the variables are discrete, then a block graph is the appropriate way to plot the data. A good block graph can be obtained from the National Lottery numbers generated each week. One Web site that will give you the latest National Lottery numbers and the numbers since the lottery began is:

Mersey World – The Lottery
```
http://lottery.merseyworld.com/Winning_index.html
```

The pupils can collect data from the last 20 lotteries and draw a pictogram of the results. This can then be compared with a pictogram of the results from all the lotteries given on:

http://lottery.merseyworld.com/Analysis/

Alternatively, the pupils could look at the weather forecast over the last five days and plot temperature and other weather statistics. This data will generate a line graph that could then be used for prediction. The weather forecast data can be found at the:

The Electronic Telegraph
http://www.telegraph.co.uk

They will need to scroll to the bottom of the page to get access to the weather page. On this page they can again scroll down to find a link to previous days' weather. Pupils can then track back as far as they think is necessary.

If you are seeking data for similar activities as those described here, then visit:

The Data and Storage Library
http://lib.stat.cmu.edu/DASL/

This is a data storage area where data is stored as 'stories'. You can click on a 'story' to get data from an array of sources. Unfortunately most of the data is collected from areas in Northern America, but you could add your own 'story' to the site thus giving it a UK flavour.

Pupil activity sheet – graph it

Every graph shows a relationship between two sets of numbers. You are asked to produce two graphs on this page that might help you generate some very useful information.

In the first graph you will produce a pictogram of the winning National Lottery numbers over the last 20 draws. You can then compare this graph with the one that shows you the trends since the National Lottery began and maybe generate a set of numbers for the next National Lottery draw.

Make a table that you can use to store the data you are collecting, then go to the following page:

http://lottery.merseyworld.com/Winning_index.html

This will give you a list of all the winning numbers over the last ten weeks that you can transfer to your table. Now plot the numbers on the left-hand axis against the number of times it appears on the bottom axis. Compare your graph to the one that shows the occurrence of numbers since the lottery began at the site:

http://lottery.merseyworld.com/Analysis/

Maybe you can now make a prediction on what numbers might come up for the next draw and see what happens. Remember that if you are under 16, you are not allowed to buy tickets.

Alternatively, what will be the temperature when the next National Lottery draw takes place? Will you need warm clothing? You can find the temperature in your region by going to the *Daily Telegraph* weather page at:

The Electronic Telegraph
http://www.telegraph.co.uk

If you scroll to the bottom of each page, you can find out what the weather was like on the previous day. Collect temperature data for the last three weeks and plot it on a graph that has the temperature on the vertical axis and the days on the horizontal axis. Use it to predict the temperature on the next National Lottery day.

Activity Maths 5 – finding pi(π)

Teacher notes

National Curriculum	Key Stage 4 Using and Applying Mathematics: 1b Shape, Space and Measure: 2b, 2e, 2f
Activity aims	To investigate the Archimedes method of finding π. To practise using the Web as a teaching resource

There are several ways in which π can be found. The most popular way is to divide the circumference by twice the radius. To do this, we get pupils to measure the circumference of various circular objects using a length of string and then divide this by the *radius × 2*. There is however another method used by Archimedes that is ideal for extension work in this area.

Archimedes took a unit circle (this could provide some interesting discussion on units) and then drew a regular polygon inside it as an attempt to determine the area of the circle. He found that the area of the polygon became closer to a constant value the more sides the polygon had. We can start by inscribing a square inside our circle of unit radius (Figure 5.6).

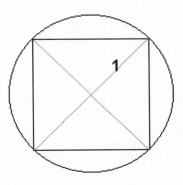

Figure 5.6 An inscribed square.

The area of one triangle can be determined as ½. As there are four triangles we have a total area of 4 × ½ = 2. If we circumscribe the square (Figure 5.7), the area of this new square is 2 × 2 = 4.

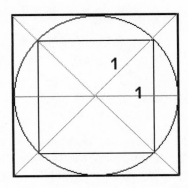

Figure 5.7 A circumscribed square.

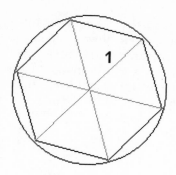

Figure 5.8 An inscribed polygon.

So we can now say that the area of the unit circle is between 2 and 4. We next do the same for a regular hexagon (Figure 5.8). For the inscribed polygon we have six equilateral triangles. One of the triangles is √¾ so the total area for the hexagon is 6 × √¾ = 2.598.

For the circumscribed polygon (Figure 5.9) we have six equilateral triangles each with an area of √1/3 so the total area is 6 × √1/3 or 6/√3 = 3.464.

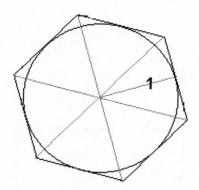

Figure 5.9 A circumscribed polygon.

The area of the circle is therefore between 2.598 and 3.464. As the number of sides of the regular polygon get larger then the value of the area gets closer to π.

This is shown on site:

Graphics for the Calculus Classroom
http://www.math.psu.edu/dna/graphics.html

which then links to:

`http://www.math.psu.edu/dna/graphics.html#archimedes`

To find out how many sides Archimedes' regular polygon had, you need to refer to his gravestone or the Web site *of Dr. Maths* where you can find the answer.

Pupil activity sheet – finding pi(π)

One way of calculating π is by finding the circumference of a circle and dividing it by *2× radius* of the circle. You will now find it in the way that Archimedes used. Go to:

`http://www.math.psu.edu/dna/graphics.html`

Move the mouse over the examples on this page until you find the *Archimedes Calculation of pi site*. Go to that site.

Look at the example there and find the area of a circle of unit radius using a four-sided, a six-sided and an eight-sided polygon inscribed within the circle. Plot the results that you have obtained on a graph. What type of graph have you got?

If you want to find out more about how Archimedes found out the value of pi, go to:

`http://forum.swarthmore.edu/dr.math/problems/`
`ferrer8.8.97.html`

where *Dr. Maths* will answer any questions you have about mathematics.

You can also search the Web using a search tool and find sites that give the value of pi to millions of decimal points.

Activity Maths 6 – Fibonacci numbers

Teacher notes

National Curriculum	Key Stage 3 Using and Applying Mathematics 1b, 4a Number: 3a, 4b
Activity aim	To examine a number series. To search the Internet and create a Web presentation

Fibonacci was born in Pisa, Italy in about 1180. He was also known as Leonardo of Pisa. His writings became influential in introducing the Indo-Arabic numeral system and making it more easily understood by scholars. His work in algebra, geometry and theoretical mathematics was far ahead of his European contemporaries.

The third part of his book *Liber abaci* (the book of the calculator) gave examples of recreational mathematical problems of the type still enjoyed today. As part of this there was a series of numbers that have become known as the Fibonacci series. This series was found to have many significant and interesting properties.

There are many Web sites that discuss Fibonacci, but the one we use here is at:

Fibonacci Numbers and Nature
`http://www.ee.surrey.ac.uk/Personal/R.Knott/Fibonacci/fibnat.html`

The activity sheet asks pupils to search for information on Fibonacci using a search tool such as Infoseek or Alta Vista (see Part 1, Chapter 2). The pupils are then directed to the site above and asked to check the flower catalogues to see if all flowers have a Fibonacci number of petals.

Any findings are to be presented in Web page format, so it might be necessary to prepare a template using a suitable software package.

Pupil activity sheet – Fibonacci numbers

You are asked to make a presentation on Fibonacci numbers in the form of a Web document. To research Fibonacci numbers use a search tool such as Alta Vista or Infoseek. Collect text and pictures from the Web and save them to either a floppy or hard disk. After researching the Web go to:

Fibonacci Numbers and Nature
`http://www.ee.surrey.ac.uk/Personal/R.Knott/Fibonacci/fibnat.html`

and, in particular, look at the petals on flowers by using the flower catalogues. See if you can find a flower that does not have a Fibonacci number of petals.

Include the answers to the questions in your presentation. The presentation will be in the form of a set of Web pages with appropriate links. Be careful about selecting the appropriate background and the font size of the text. To ensure that your pages display quickly, try to avoid too many pictures on one page.

ENGLISH

Introduction

The Web can provide access to numerous sites of interest to the English teacher and the number of sites continues to grow. These sites either relate specifically to English study or can be looked at as examples of the use of language. Email facilities that have become available through access to the Internet are another valuable resource as they considerably widen the communication possibilities.

An important site for the English teacher is one that gives pathways to other valuable resources. The National Council for Educational Technology page at:

IT in English
`http://www.ngfl.gov.uk/resource/cits/english/link.html`

is part of an IT in English project and has some valuable links to sites for English Teachers interested in IT, sites for writers, early English sites, classic literature sites and other language study sites.

For the busy Key Stage 3/4 teacher the site run by Harry Dodds is a definite bookmark. Find it at:

English Teaching in the United Kingdom
`http://ourworld.compuserve.com/homepages/Harry_Dodds/`

How can English and the use of the Web link with IT capability? Word processing and desktop publishing software is probably the most common form of IT used in the classroom. All pupils are now expected to present a document produced with a word processing package.

In English, it is the process of reading, researching, structuring, drafting and editing the word processed document that is of importance. These processes can be enhanced by the integration of the Web. The Web gives access to more up-to-date research material in graphic and text form, and provides a non-paper medium for presenting work in a hypertext format.

The activities below are examples of how the Web could be integrated in its various forms into parts of the English curriculum. There are activities that use the Web for information-gathering, communicating and presenting work at different levels of English and IT capability. The activities have no set time allocation and can be used in a variety of ways.

Activity English 1 – producing a play

Teacher notes

National Curriculum	Key Stage 4 Speaking and Listening: 1a, 1c, 2a Reading: 1b, 1d
Activity aims	To investigate the process of play production. To use the Web as an information source

In this exercise pupils work in groups. They are to imagine that they are part of a production team that is bidding to produce a play. Each group will be asked to present plans for the production of one scene of a Shakespeare play in an attempt to gain the contract to produce the new play. In the plans, consideration must be given to the important elements of the production such as set, costumes, soundtrack, actors and actresses, special effects and budget.

Pupils must become intimate with the text and allow their imagination to create the best possible production, within budget and time restraints. The scene that will be used is the balcony scene from Romeo and Juliet. This is available on the Web in several places.

University of Victoria English Dept.
`http://www.engl.uvic.ca/faculty/MBHomePage/`
`ISShakespeare/Rom/Rom2.2.html`

or:

University of Sydney, Australia
`http://www.gh.cs.usyd.edu.au/~matty/Shakespeare/texts/`
`tragedies/romeoandjuliet_2.html#xref010`

As part of the research for the project the pupils can search for set construction and lighting plans for plays on the Web. This will need some careful keyword searching using one of the search tools (see Part 1, Chapter 2). The page below has some useful notes associated with the text:

Bruce Spielbauer's page
`http://emiko.igcom.net/~bruce/rom22.html`

The pupils can be allowed artistic license with the scene. They might get some useful ideas from accessing the Web pages that look at the film of Romeo and Juliet. The production groups can deliver the proposals orally.

Pupil activity sheet – producing a play

You are a production team who is bidding to produce a play. The company who is financing the play has asked all the bidders to produce plans for a scene from Romeo and Juliet and they will use this plan as the basis for selecting the production team for their play. Your task is to plan the production of the balcony scene from Shakespeare's Romeo and Juliet.

You can find, and print out, the text for the scene on:

```
http://www.engl.uvic.ca/faculty/MBHomePage/
ISShakespeare/Rom/Rom2.2.html
```

In your plan consider the set location, actresses and actors, music costumes, prompts, etc. You will be expected to show evidence that you have used the Web in this planning period and completed some detailed searches.

To arrange the production details you must know the play well. The following page has some useful notes on different aspects of the scene:

```
http://emiko.igcom.net/~bruce/rom22.html
```

Try and make some estimate of the cost of the different elements of the production process as the successful group will probably be one of the most cost effective in this limited budget production.

Use your imagination to create the best possible production. You might find some useful ideas if you access Web sites that review the film of Romeo and Juliet.

Activity English 2 – masculine or feminine?

Teacher notes

National Curriculum	Key Stage 3 and 4 Speaking and Listening: 3b Reading: 3b
Activity aims	To develop an understanding of grammar. To use the Web to find information

Ask your pupils to make a list of nouns, verbs, adjectives and adverbs which have a distinct masculine or feminine meaning linked to them. For some background reading on this go to the Purdue Online Writing Lab's Non-Sexist language page at:

`http://owl.english.purdue.edu/Files/26.html`

The pupils are then asked to examine the poem 'Filling Station' by Elizabeth Bishop at:

`http://www.cwrl.utexas.edu/~daniel/bishop/poetry/`
`fillingstation/fillingstation.html`

Filling Station
Oh, but it is dirty!
– this little filling station,
oil-soaked, oil permeated,
to a disturbing, over all
black translucency.
Be careful with that match!

Father wears a dirty,
oil soaked monkey suit
that cuts him under the arms,
and several quick and saucy
and greasy sons assist him
(it's a family filling station),
all quite thoroughly dirty.

Do they live in the station?
It has a cement porch
behind the pumps, and on it
a set of crushed and grease-
impregnated wickerwork;
on the wicker sofa
a dirty dog, quite comfy.

Some comic books provide
the only note of color –
of certain color. They lie
upon a big dim doily
draping a taboret
(part of the set), beside
a big hirsute begonia.

Why the extraneous plant?
Why the taboret?
Why, oh why, the doily?
(Embroidered in daisy stitch
with marguerites, I think,
and heavy with gray crochet.)

Somebody embroidered the doily.
Somebody waters the plant,
or oils it, maybe. Somebody
arranges the rows of cans
so that they softly say:
ESSO–SO–SO–SO
to high strung automobiles.
Somebody loves us all.

(Elizabeth Bishop)

Bishop makes many references to 'femininity' and defines 'masculinity' without being obvious or condemnatory. Ask the pupils to determine who is the 'somebody' that takes care of the flowers and '. . . loves us all'.

The pupils are then invited to examine a national online electronic newspaper like the *Daily Telegraph* at:

The Electronic Telegraph
http://www.telegraph.co.uk

and see how sexist language is used in the newspaper articles.

Pupil activity sheet – masculine or feminine?

Some words have a distinct feminine or masculine meaning linked to them. Make a list that gives at least five examples of nouns, verbs, adjectives and adverbs that are distinctly feminine or masculine. When your list is complete go to:

http://owl.english.purdue.edu/Files/26.html

This site will give you some background reading on non-sexist language and allow you to compare your answers to the examples given there. Now go to, and examine, the poem 'Filling Station' by Elizabeth Bishop at:

http://www.cwrl.utexas.edu/~daniel/bishop/poetry/
fillingstation/fillingstation.html

and see how references to femininity and masculinity have been made in this poem. Who is the 'somebody' that takes care of the flowers and '. . . loves us all.'? Make notes of your answer. When you have finished, go to a national online daily newspaper, say the *Telegraph* or *Guardian* and see if you can find examples of sexist language being used. Print any articles that you wish to comment on.

You will be expected to report back on what you have found out and write a short paragraph on your findings.

Activity English 3 – chase the semicolon

Teacher notes

National Curriculum	Key Stage 3 Writing: 3b
Activity aims	To develop grammar and sentence construction. To interact with the Web and communicate using the Internet

Grammar and sentence constructions are important elements of English at Key Stage 3 and 4. To support grammar work there are some very good sites where examples and definitions can be accessed.

One such site by Anthony Hughes is particularly good and this can be found at:

Online English Grammar
http://www.go-ed.com/english/grammar/

There are also several sites in America and Canada where the spelling can be a little different but the grammar is the same. One of the best is at:

University of Calgary English Department
http://www.ucalgary.ca/hu/ENGL/Grammar/punctuation.htm

The activity sheet guides pupils to a grammar quiz at:
http://www.go-ed.com/english/practice/rside/G_quizq.html

The questions in the quiz are given in the activity sheet so that pupils can prepare answers using the reference sites if needed. After completing the quiz, pupils can go to the quiz site and receive instant feedback on whether their answers are correct or not.

Pupils are then asked to go to the Lydbury English Centre where they can create a personal profile about themselves and enter the centre as users.

The address of the centre is:

Lydbury English Centre
http://www.go-ed.com:8080/~3/

The personal profile contains information on the pupils email address and a log-on name that is different from their own.

Their log-on name will appear when they contribute to the forum. Pupils can now contribute to other activities on the site including the competitions and maybe add to the trivia page. They can check some of the questions relating to English grammar that may have arisen during the quiz, or formulate a question about English grammar to submit to the forum.

This will give them an insight into the use of the Web as a communication medium. Conference pages are important ways of communicating on the Internet and this is one of many.

Pupils could contribute to other forums, some of which can be accessed through the Research Machines Internet for Learning site at:

Research Machines Internet for Learning
http://www.eduweb.org.uk

There is also the possibility of pupils contributing to UseNet newsgroups (see Part 1, Chapter 4).

Finally, a punctuation quiz can be found at:

The Mining Company
http://kidswriting.miningco.com/msubrgrm.htm

Pupil activity sheet – chase the semicolon

This is an activity about English grammar so find out what you already know by trying to answer the questions in the grammar quiz (see below). If you have any problems go to:

http://www.go-ed.com/english/grammar/

The grammar quiz
Decide if the following sentences are true or false:

1. There is no future tense in English.
2. The train leaves at 7.00 pm.
   This is an acceptable sentence referring to the future.
3. You are visiting a friend's house. Your host says
   'Will you stay for lunch'?
   This means he or she is asking about your plans for the future.
4. Will, must, may, might, would, shall.
   These are all examples of modal verbs.
5. Modal verbs can never be followed by an infinitive with 'to'.
6. 'I'm going' is an example of the present continuous tense.
7. 'I've gone' is an example of the past continuous tense.
8. In the sentence:
   Sharon kicked the dog.
   The word 'kicked' is a transitive verb.
9. In the sentence
   The sun set in the west.
   The word 'set' is an intransitive verb.
10. These sentences all contain examples of the passive:
    This garment should be dry-cleaned.
    I wasn't told about the meeting until this morning.
    They would have been hurt if they'd been going any faster.
    I could have gone to the play but I didn't want to.

When you think you have the answers go to the following site and check them:

http://www.go-ed.com/english/practice/rside/G_quizq.html

Are you still uncertain about a particular answer? Then go to the Lydbury English Centre at:

http://www.go-ed.com:8080/~3/

To gain access to this site you will have to register. This is not uncommon on the Web, so if you have not done it before, this will be good practice.

To enter the Centre as users you will need to create a personal profile. Be prepared to leave your email address and a user name that is different from your own real name. Once you are a member, you can ask questions about English grammatical rules.

Finally, browse the site and see if there are any other areas of discussion that you would like to contribute to.

Activity English 4 – choose your own adventure

Teacher notes

National Curriculum	Key Stage 3 Writing: 1a, 1b, 2b
Activity aims	To provide a context for creative writing. To examine the structure of Web pages

There are many sites on the Web where you can choose your own adventure. All you need is to use a search tool (see Part 1, Chapter 2) and the phrase 'choose your own adventure'.

Many hundreds of options will be listed because you have not only ventured into the world of storytelling but also into the world of computer games like Dungeons and Dragons. Most of the storytelling sites are in North America, and with their language and spelling they are not necessarily suitable for a pupil in the UK. No doubt there will be some UK sites emerging soon.

Pupils are asked to visit the site below where they can find an adventure story that could have many endings. The challenge is to find all the endings. An even greater challenge is for pupils to create their own story with a variety of endings which can then be placed on a school Intranet or even published on the Web itself.

The adventure below has been chosen as a good example because pupils of Key Stage 3 age group have developed it. The story can be found at the Hillside Elementary School's Web site:

Hillside Elementary School
`http://hillside.coled.umn.edu/class1/Buzz/Story.html`

The Hillside site has a random ending generator that picks an ending, completely at random, for pupils to view.

Copy and paste the story from the Hillside site into a word processor. Your pupils can then insert it into a set of Web pages that will be the home for alternative endings generated. The activity sheet asks pupils to generate an ending to this story. The story and endings can then be converted into a Web page using a Web authoring tool.

A development of this would be for the pupils to create their own start to an adventure and then a set of alternative endings. If you have the facilities, you could then publish the adventure and its alternative endings on the Web or school Intranet.

Pupil activity sheet – choosing your own adventure

Go to site:
`http://hillside.coled.umn.edu/class1/Buzz/Story.html`

and read the story. What ending do you think it might have?

Try using the random ending generator to find some alternative endings already suggested by other pupils. If the random ending generator is not working, try and write your own ending in a word processing program and submit it to your teacher.

The ending could be published on your own Internet Web pages so that others may access it. Make sure that all the spelling and grammar is correct before submitting your work.

Activity English 5 – an online encyclopedia

Teacher notes

National Curriculum	Key Stage 3 Reading: 1f, 2c, 3b
Activity aims	To create a set of resources in the form of an encyclopedia. To learn how to handle information and produce a Web presentation

This activity focuses on developing pupils' information-handling skills. The activity can be completed as a class activity and involves accessing the Web, CD-ROMs, books, pamphlets and other information sources to complete a resource file on a particular topic.

The resource file will be part of an ongoing encyclopedia of information that will be continually updated. It can be published as Web pages either on the class computer, school Intranet or the Web itself.

As part of this exercise pupils can access the Encyclopedia Britannica in its short version, or enrol using their email address for seven days free trial.

Encyclopedia Britannica
`http://www.eb.com/`

Pupils will have to be familiar with the different search tools and how to use them because of the need to access information from other sources (see Part 1, Chapter 2).

It will be necessary to give pupils instructi
Web pages and their design including the standa.
as text and colours across different pages (see Pa

Pupil activity sheet – an online enc

Your teacher will give your group a topic that will resul
of an online encyclopedia. The encyclopedia will be   ..in of a
Web site. It will therefore consist of a number of linkeu pages.

Visit the Encyclopedia Britannica site at:

```
http://www.eb.com/
```

Look at how an encyclopedia is structured. Look at the way that hypertext is used to link words to other pages, which in turn give further information, and study the way in which pictures are used. Take note of the way in which you can return to the original text from where you started out.

To help with the success of the project you may need to organize your group. A suggested group structure is:

Director   –   responsible for making sure that all the group in the production are working towards the same objective.
Researcher   –   responsible for finding out information about the topic.
Story writer –   responsible for constructing the storyboard, requesting information and overseeing production.
Producer   –   responsible for producing the story on the screen.

For information on your topic, you will need to search the Web using a search tool such as Yahoo or Excite. Save any relevant pictures and text that you want to use in your encyclopedia. Decide how you would like to present your encyclopedia. How will users find their way round the encyclopedia? What links will you make?

GEOGRAPHY

Introduction

Geography is well represented on the Internet and the Web in particular. A lot of organizations have details of their economic and development activities published on Web pages. You will find many local authorities in the UK offering a wide range of useful information that can be used

...opment and economic geography. Physical geography has a ...ty of sites dealing with weather and volcanoes in many different ...rts of the world and these can be easily found using the search facilities available to you (see Part 1, Chapter 2).

Pupils studying geography can use the Web to:

- enhance their skills of geographical inquiry and investigation
- gain access to a wide range of geographical knowledge and information sources
- experience alternative images of people, places and environment.

A useful reference page for the geographer is the Geography IT support page on the Virtual Teacher Centre (VTC) site:

Virtual Teacher Centre
http://vtc.ngfl.gov.uk/resource/cits/geog/index.html

This page gives you the main links to other geography resources such as the World Factbook that gives the reader access to geographical, economic and social information about each country in the world. This would be particularly useful for Key Stage 4 work on population studies.

Another useful site is an American one at:

Geography – The Mining Company
http://geography.miningco.com/

This site has a lot of detailed US statistics as well as world population pyramids.

The two examples of activities in this section both involve pupils in using the Web and its interactive capability.

Activity Geography 1 – following the voyage

Teacher notes

National Curriculum	Key Stage 3 Geographical skills: e, g, h Places
Activity aims	To develop map-reading skills. To practise the interactive use of Web pages

ɔ activity uses an excellent Web resource. The Parc.Xerox is an ɪeractive map of the world. The map enables the geographer to use ɪɪap references of longitude and latitude values to plot the progress of a variety of voyages including those by sea, air or land. The map is on:

Xerox. Map Viewer
http://pubweb.parc.xerox.com/map

A voyage that could be used is by explorer Tim Severin. During January 1996 Tim and his crew retraced the path of Alfred Russell Wallace, who along with Charles Darwin, first announced the theory of natural selection. Their account of the voyage is found at:

http://wvw.curriculumweb.org/cw/ercntr/spiceislands/sivoyage/spiceisl.html

Alternatively, pupils are asked to search for other voyages like yacht races or balloon trips on the Web. Some yacht races give regular position updates and you might be lucky enough to hit a live online yacht race. The Whitbread yacht race is an annual event and has a web site at :

http://www.whitbread.org/diary/index.html

It is also possible to get archived information on a race that has already been run. For example the Transpac Honolulu race has the history of the race archived on:

http://krypton.nmr.hawaii.edu/transpac/95/pos_rpts.html

All of these races visit various places and a study of these can be an extension of this activity. Pupils will need to be familiar with the Parc Xerox interactive map. There are tutorials available at the map site or on the Spice Islands' site. The pupil activity sheet attempts to give the necessary instructions for the successful completion of this activity.

Pupil activity sheet – following the voyage

In this activity you will follow the progress of a voyage and try to trace the route that it takes. You will first have to find a suitable voyage that gives you regular updates on its position. To do this you will have to search the Web.

Search using the keywords 'yacht races' or 'balloon circumnavigation'. It would be exciting if a race is in progress but if this is not possible you could go to a site like:

`http://krypton.nmr.hawaii.edu/transpac/95/pos_rpts.html`

Another site where you might find progress reports, which include the position of boats, is the Whitbread site that is the home of the Whitbread Around the World Yacht Race race.

`http://www.whitbread.org/diary/index.html`

The voyage now needs to be plotted on a map. A suitable map can be found at:

`http://pubweb.parc.xerox.com/map`

This is an interactive map and your success at using it will depend on your understanding of longitude and latitude and of the structure of Web pages.

Using the Parc Xerox interactive map

You can select an area of the map and, by clicking on it, obtain an enlargement of that area. If you look at the top of the map you find the latitude–longitude values for the view that you have selected. Now look in the URL box of your browser and you will notice that this figure is included in the URL. You can change these values in the URL and press Enter to see how the map will now refocus on the longitude and latitude values that you have selected (Figure 5.10).

`http://pubweb.parc.xerox.com/map/ht=22.50/lat=48.31/`
`lon=-12.59/wd=45.00`

You can mark your latitude and longitude value by going to the *Options* section on the Parc Xerox map page. Note that you now get another address(Figure 5.11):

`http://pubweb.parc.xerox.com/map/ht=22.50/lat=48.31/`
`lon=-12.59/mark=38.31,-12.59/wd=45.00`

The information about the mark can be changed in the same way that you changed the latitude and longitude in the previous example – by using the URL box. This allows you to position the mark at the exact position of the voyage. The map can be printed out at any time.

When you have finished plotting the voyage of the yacht use the search tools to find out some interesting geographical data on one of the places visited during the voyage.

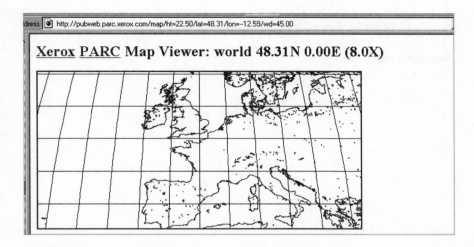

Figure 5.10   The longitude and latitude map.

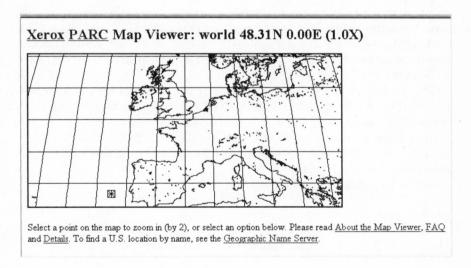

Figure 5.11   Marking a longitude and latitude map.

Activity Geography 2 – exploring volcanoes

Teacher notes

National Curriculum	Key Stage 3 Tectonic Processes: a, b or c, d or e Places
Activity aims	To understand ideas on volcanoes and their impact on societies. To use the Web as a source of information.

There is a lot of up-to-date information on the Web on earthquakes and volcanoes. One common approach to studying such phenomena is to use case study material. This seems an ideal topic to approach through interaction with the Web.

The activity can be structured as a group activity where each group is given the role of scientific 'human interest' reporters who have to report on the cause and location of earthquakes and volcanoes in a particular area of the world. Pupils will have to search the Web to obtain information on the communities affected by volcanic activity (see Part 1, Chapter 2).

The geographical areas of the world that you can allocate to the pupils are Africa, North America, North Asia, Central and South America, Antarctica, Europe and West Asia and South East Asia.

Information on volcanoes and earthquakes can be found at Volcano World, a site that has an online volcanologist to answer all those unanswerable questions.

Access to Volcano World is via:

```
http://volcano.und.edu/new_index.html
```

This site will also provide links to many other areas of interest.

Pupil activity sheet – exploring volcanoes

You are part of a group who will be compiling a report for a national newspaper on volcanic activity in a part of the world and its effects upon the local population. Your teacher will give you the geographical area you will be studying.

You can access information on the area by contacting:

```
http://volcano.und.edu/new_index.html
```

You may need to use a search tool on the Web (see Part 1, Chapter 2) to find some more information about the communities that are affected by volcanic activity.

You will provide a 500-word article about the volcanoes and communities. In this preparation you could ask questions to the volcanologist who can be contacted via Volcano World. As an additional task to test your knowledge about volcanoes, you could try the quiz in the box below, which can also be found on the Volcano World pages.

What is the name for the group of volcanoes that occur around the Pacific Ocean?

Circle of Stones
Ring of Fire
Ocean Edge Volcanoes

The largest volcanoes on Earth (and Mars and Venus too) are:

strato-volcanoes
cinder cones
shield volcanoes

The biggest historic eruption in the USA was at:

Mauna Loa
Mt. St. Helens
Novarupta

Scientists monitor volcanic activity using:

seismometers
tea leaves
spy satellites

The most common type of volcanic rock is:

andesite
pumice
basalt

Magma is made in the Earth's:

crust
mantle
core

Lava flows that have smooth and ropy surfaces are called:

aa
blocky
pahoehoe

A volcano that has not erupted for many years, but is likely to erupt sometime in the future, is called:

lazy
dormant
extinct

Most strato-volcanoes are located above plate tectonic:

subduction zones
hot spots
down ramps

The largest volcano on Earth is:

St. Helens
Dante's Peak
Mauna Loa

To find the answers to these questions go to Volcano World.

HISTORY

Introduction

There are many sites on the Web for the aspiring historian. The sites mainly give factual information and the best of these is the Encyclopedia Britannica, a shortened version of which is available online. This site can provide brief answers to many questions of fact. For more detailed answers the historian will have to subscribe to the full version of 'Online Britannica' or purchase the CD which, like the Web, uses a Web browser as its front end. There is the possibility of using a seven-days' free trial option of the full version if you have a valid email address.

For the historian, the ability to use the search tools of the Web (see Part 1, Chapter 2) is a necessary skill and an important part of historical inquiry. Pupils should be aware of the different ways in which the search tools can be used and how hard copies of printed sources, pictures and photographs can be obtained from Web pages.

The following activities aim to illustrate the way in which access to the Web can be successfully incorporated into the History curriculum.

Activity History 1 – timelines

Teacher notes

National Curriculum	Key Stage 3 Key Elements: 1a, 1b, 3a, 3b, 5a, 5b, 5c Study Unit: 2d
Activity aims	To develop ideas on timelines. To investigate the use of the Web in history

There are some useful history sites that give access to information in a way that is appropriate for Key Stage 3 history students. The Hyper History site, which is featured in this activity sheet, is an excellent example of the use of hypertext in documentation. The hypertext links take you to photographs of people, and pictures and maps of places of interest.

Hyper History
http://www.hyperhistory.com/

The Hyper History site is built around the concept of a timeline and this gives the framework for this activity.

Pupils are asked to select a period in history and compare different interpretations of that period. In this instance, it is suggested that the *Thirty Years War* be used. Pupils are asked to go to the Hyper History site and the timeline produced there to extract relevant information. The Hyper History site is an American site and the interpretations of events may be different from that of a British source so pupils are then asked to go to the Encyclopedia Britannica site:

Encyclopedia Britannica
http://www.eb.com/search/

to a CD-ROM like *History of the World* by Dorling Kindersley, or to a textbook and find information on the same event. The task is to reconcile the differences and create a timeline for that event which pupils think is appropriate. The timeline could be presented as a Web document if the appropriate Web software is available.

Pupil activity sheet – timelines

It is important to realize that the interpretations of events are dependent on the perspectives of the interpreter. This activity asks you to select different interpretations of one event from a variety of sources and to analyse the similarities and differences. You can then create your own timeline of the event.

The event is the 'Thirty Years War'. You can get information on this from an American source on the Web by using the Hyper History timeline at:

http://www.hyperhistory.com/

To achieve this you need to go to the main page and first select the 'History' option, then select the appropriate period for the 'Thirty Years War' by identifying it on the timeline. You do this by moving the mouse arrow to the period required and clicking on it. This should take you to information that is shown in the right-hand box of the screen (Figure 5.12). Print out this information.

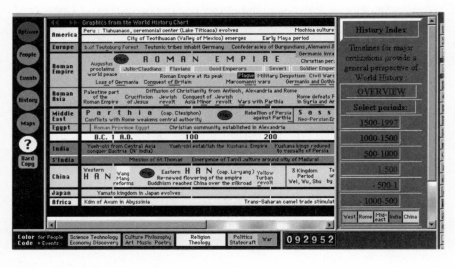

Figure 5.12 The timeline.

For an alternative set of information go to the Encyclopedia Britannica site where you will be able to access brief notes on the same event.

http://www.eb.com/search/

If you are completing this activity as part of a long-term research activity then you could register for a seven-days' free trial of the full version of Britannica online and get access to a more detailed set of information on the event.

Alternatively, you could search for information using a Web search tool, access a CD-ROM such as the Dorling Kindersley 'History of the World' or consult an appropriate textbook.

The kind of information you could search for includes:

- the reasons that led to the start of the war
- the start and finish dates of the war
- the geographical area(s) where it took place
- the periods of fighting and the dates of these periods
- who gained what and who lost what in the war.

Make hard copies of the information and note the similarities and differences. Decide on how you are going to tackle inconsistencies in the information and construct a timeline for the *Thirty Years War* based upon your analysis.

Activity History 2 – coalmines, women and children in Victorian times

Teacher notes

National Curriculum	Key Stage 3 Key Elements: 4a, 4b, 5a, 5b, 5c Study unit 3: 1b
Activity aims	To learn how to examine for bias in historical evidence and to practise accessing information on the Web

This activity takes text from parliamentary documents about the conditions in coalmines in the first half of the nineteenth century. Pupils access this information and download it to a word processing file. The pupils can then analyse the information and highlight words and phrases that express feelings or bias about conditions in the mines.

The site they will be using is called The Victorian Web and it contains a wealth of information about Victorian times. The site address is:

```
http://www.stg.brown.edu/projects/hypertext/landow/
victorian/victov.html
```

Pupils examine the highlighted text and determine the factual basis for the beliefs and feelings of the witnesses. They then arrange the statements by theme, for example, by the treatment of children and women or by the hours worked. This could be done within the word processing program. Make sure that pupils have access to instructions on using search tools before starting this activity (see Part 1, Chapter 2).

Pupil activity sheet – coalmines, women and children in Victorian times

This activity is asking you to examine the text of evidence submitted in the early nineteenth century on the conditions of labour for women and children. You are to look for evidence of bias in the factual statements of witnesses as found at the Victorian Page Web site:

```
http://www.stg.brown.edu/projects/hypertext/landow/
victorian/victov.html
```

Remember! If you find that the site is no longer at that address (URL), you can try to track it by going to the root directory (see Part 1, Chapter 1) which in this case is:

```
http://www.stg.brown.edu/
```

Find evidence on 'child labour' in coalmines, which is in the section labelled *Testimony Gathered by Ashley's Mines Commission,* and download the information to your word processing package on your hard disk.

Examine the text and highlight all parts of the evidence that you believe express opinions based on historical fact and support a particular point of view.

Collect all the phrases supporting one view and cut and paste them into a separate document. Do a similar exercise for the statements expressing the opposing view.

Repeat the whole exercise for 'women in coalmines', using the same source.

If you are not satisfied with the information on this site, use the search tools to search the Web for further information. Read carefully the instructions on using your search tool (see Part 1, Chapter 2).

Try and find out what was the true state of conditions in mines and collieries in the nineteenth century.

DESIGN AND TECHNOLOGY

Introduction

The study of Design and Technology looks forward to the future but recognizes that the present is based on the achievements of the past. The ideas of the present are important for moulding the future. Increasingly, designers need to be able to access large amounts of knowledge before developing a design proposal, and manufacturers need to sell their products and ideas in very competitive markets.

The Web is an information base that is fast becoming a record of past designs and a repository of ideas for the future. It offers a unique up-to-date source of statistics, marketing and designing ideas, and information on raw materials.

Like other areas of the National Curriculum, there are sites that provide information and useful links for technology teachers. In the UK, there is the VTC (Virtual Teacher Centre) Design and Technology page at:

Virtual Teacher Centre
`http://vtc.ngfl.gov.uk/resource/cits/dant/index.html`

and two other sites at:

University of Central England
`http://www.uce.ac.uk/education/cript/information.html`

and at:
`http://www.technologyindex.com/education/`

It is already possible to see examples of how the facilities offered by the Web and the Internet are being used to advantage. For example, schools are linking with local universities and colleges of further education to take advantage of the engineering CAM facilities of higher and further education. Product designs, produced by school pupils, are downloaded to the CAM equipment at the universities and colleges of further education and the production process observed by pupils via a video link across the Internet.

The two activities in this section of the book are provided to give a flavour of how the Internet and the Web can be used in the design and technology lesson.

Activity Technology 1 – promoting a product

Teacher notes

National Curriculum	Key Stage 3 and 4 Designing skills: 3a Products and applications: 8e Quality: 9a
Activity aims	To develop ideas on promoting a product. Learning how to design and create Web pages

The promotion of an artefact or an idea in commerce and industry is often through some form of presentation to potential financial backers. Such presentations have invariably involved IT in some form. It is now likely that a presentation will have a multimedia element and use presentation software like Microsoft *PowerPoint*. Looking to the future the influence of the Web will become increasingly important and Web browsers will become a major promotion and publicity medium.

This activity asks pupils to create a multimedia presentation for a variety of audiences using a Web browser as the presentation format. The objective is to sell an artefact or idea to the audiences.

Pupils will need access to scanners, digital cameras and appropriate graphics software such as Paint Shop Pro (see Part 1, Chapter 4). They will also need a Web authoring package. You might like to consider using a program such as Microsoft *FrontPage* or Adobe *PageMill* to construct your web pages (see Part1, Chapter 3).

Pupils will need to spend some time searching the Web for resources and ideas. This will mean that they should be familiar with the search tools (see Part 1, Chapter 2). You will find that phrases such as 'Selling through the Internet' will generate sites that could lead to further research.

Access to pictures and sounds on the Web, including animated GIFs and page backgrounds, can also be obtained through the use of search tools.

Pupil activity sheet – promoting a product

This task asks you to promote an artefact or an idea on the Web. Your initial task is to choose a product or an idea to promote. Then you need to search the Web for ideas or artefacts similar to the one you have chosen and determine the potential customer base with respect to users of the Web. You can find out about Web users by looking at the results of Web surveys available on the Internet. Use the search tools to find them.

Using this research information, you can create two multimedia design proposals for Web pages, one each for a different audience of Web users.

Following the design proposal, you can construct the two promotional Web presentations. You can use any material in your promotion. To assist you in this, you can use any available scanners, digital cameras and sound recording equipment and, of course, the Web itself as a potential source of material.

Each Web page will consist of hyperlinks to other pages and it is expected that the presentation will consist of at least ten pages. Remember that pictures that are very large can take a long time to load and the average Web user will only spend a few seconds on a page if they are not immediately interested in the look and content.

Activity Technology 2 – sending messages

Teacher notes

National Curriculum	Key Stage 3 Systems and Control: 6a, 6c, 6e, 6g
Activity aims	To examine the principles of digital communication. To use the Web as a teaching resource

For this activity each group of pupils will require a battery, lightbulb, lightbulb holder, wires and a switch. The work in this activity involves the use of one of the first online science/technology textbooks 'Science in Action'. The aims of 'Science in Action' are:

● to explore the world of domestic electronic appliances
● to introduce important themes from the Science and Design and Technology curricula in an interesting and motivating way
● to provide classroom-tested, ready-to-use material requiring the minimum of preparation.

The project site is at:

Science in Action
http://www.tcns.co.uk/philips/scact10.html

The Science in Action project offers a simple introduction to the technological, scientific, environmental and design aspect of electronics together with a structured set of classroom activities. Although aimed at Key Stage 2, it can be easily adapted for Key Stage 3 work.

Pupils are asked to access the 'Science in Action' site and obtain a plan for the equipment to be used. The simple light circuit is then used as a communication tool to transmit Morse Code. As an extension activity pupils could be asked to search for information on codes and coding.

After completing the Morse Code exercise pupils are asked to communicate with each other using a digital code (1s and 0s). This is the code that is used in a Fax machine. The code can be transmitted using the same apparatus used in the Morse activity. A '1' could be represented by a long flash of light while a '0' by a short flash. Pupils are asked to use the digital code to 'fax' a message (a picture) across the room.

After the picture has been 'faxed' the focus of the rest of the activity is an evaluation of this technique of transmitting a message and ways by which it can be improved.

Pupil activity page – sending messages

Go to the following page:
http://www.tcns.co.uk/philips/scact10.html

Select the option *Communications* and go to that page.

Using the equipment that is available to you, construct the circuit shown in the diagram. Now devise a short message of six words, and using 'Morse Code' send a signal to another group on the other side of the room using the light source. You will have to decide what type of signal corresponds to a *dash* and a *dot* that make up the Morse Code (Figure 5.13).

Instead of sending a coded signal using Morse, you are now going to pretend that you are a fax machine and are going to send a message using a digital code. Draw a picture in the grid below (Figure 5.14) and transmit it across the room. Decide on which part of the picture you are going to start with and then work from right to left. For every square that is shaded, since it contains part of your picture, display a long flash of light. A short flash of light represents an unshaded square.

When you have finished sending signals and recording the message, join the other group and discuss the quality of the picture received and the method by which the information was transferred. Can you improve upon it using equipment that is available to you in the classroom? Produce a plan of your improved communication method.

Morse Code

a	• -	n	- •
b	- • • •	o	- - -
c	- • - •	p	• - - •
d	- • •	q	- - • -
e	•	r	• - •
f	• • - •	s	• • •
g	- - •	t	-
h	• • • •	u	• • -
i	• •	v	• • • -
j	• - - -	w	• - -
k	- • -	x	- • • -
l	• - • •	y	- • - -
m	- -	z	- - • •
1	• - - - -	6	- • • • •
2	• • - - -	7	- - • • •
3	• • • - -	8	- - - • •
4	• • • • -	9	- - - - •
5	• • • • •	0	- - - - -

Figure 5.13   Morse code.

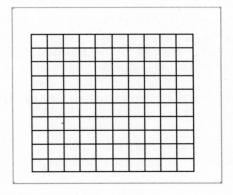

Figure 5.14   Grid.

MODERN LANGUAGES

A series of broad issues for modern language teachers were identified in a recent document on IT and modern language teaching (http://vtc.ngfl.gov.uk/resource/cits/mfl/). These start from the basis that all pupils are entitled to use IT to:

- communicate in the target language
- communicate with people of the target languages and communities
- develop and improve all four language skills
- enhance their language-learning skills, eg to develop their understanding of underlying structures
- develop or enhance independent learning skills
- access a range of resources in the target language and identify with the people of target language communities and countries
- meet their special needs for access to language learning
- make effective use of and extend existing IT capability.

The use of the Internet with its communication and information facilities can contribute to all these entitlements.

The Web is particularly useful because of its world-wide basis. There are sites for most European cities where it is possible to get a wealth of multimedia information in the home language. The sites will provide information on the commercial and cultural aspects of the city and its environs as well as contact names. Contact names will provide the user with the other important Internet resource – communication with the target country.

There are several sites that must be visited by the modern language teacher as they provide valuable routes to other important sites and resources on the Web. The CTI Centre for Modern Languages at Hull University is an important resource including a list of specialist search tools for the language teacher to search sites within a target country. Another useful site is the Virtual Language Centre. These sites are at:

Hull CTI
http://www.hull.ac.uk/cti/
Virtual Language Centre
http://www.becta.org.uk/linguanet/

The activities illustrate how the Internet can be incorporated into the modern language curriculum.

Activity Modern Language 1 – the music we like

Teacher notes

National Curriculum	
Activity aims	To use the Internet for communication and publishing

Note: there is no pupil activity sheet for this activity.

Pupils will need access to a Web page template. They will need to establish communication with a school in the target country. This can be accomplished by using an organization such as European Schools Online at:

http://www.eun.org/contact/

At this site you will find almost 600 schools which are online and may be interested in becoming involved with your project. Pupils will have to email the schools and ask them if they would like to participate.

The next stage is the construction of a questionnaire in the target language asking about musical tastes. The questionnaire is then emailed as an attached document to the target country schools and the results are subsequently incorporated into an article on musical tastes published as Web pages.

Depending upon the information communication capability of the pupils the web pages could contain audio elements (see Part 1, Chapter 3).

Activity Modern Language 2 – a multilingual web

Teacher notes

National Curriculum	Key Stage 3 Communicating information and handling information
Activity aims	To use the Internet for publishing

Note: there is no pupil activity sheet with this activity.

This is a group activity. Access to Web page templates using a suitable software package such as Microsoft FrontPage will be needed. A digital camera and scanner will also be required.

In this activity pupils are asked to prepare presentation material on their school and locality in one of the modern languages taught in their school.

As a group activity it is suggested that the pupils adopt specific roles within the group. One possible structure is:

Director – responsible for making sure that all those involved in the production are working towards the same objective.

Researcher – responsible for finding out information that will be included on the pages.

Story writer – responsible for constructing the storyboard, requesting information and overseeing production.

Translator – responsible for checking on the translation of the site.

Producer – responsible for producing the story on the screen.

As part of the preparation pupils should access other European school Web pages and their own localities' Web site so that sources of material can be researched. Other School Web sites can be found using:

http://www.eun.org/contact/

The Web site of their locality can usually be found by using:

CityNet
http://www.city.net/

This site will lead you to the sites of all the European cities and from these the surrounding locality.

When the initial research has been completed pupils can then construct a storyboard for their Web site, collect the pictures and text, and insert these into the web template.

MUSIC

Introduction

Note: this section contains no specific pupil activities.

Most modern musicians have their own Web pages and a lot of their followers have developed pages that link to their work. Orchestras have performed live on the Internet and musical scores are readily available.

More importantly, Web pages are being used for publishing and discussing compositions composed by pupils.

Music has well-established links to electronics and the production of digital music files is now commonplace. It is therefore a small step to link the production of digital sound to Web pages.

If you want to listen to a lot of the music you will find that it is necessary to download the Real Audio Software (see Part 1, Chapter 3). This is an ideal piece of software to download because it requires no decompression software at the end of the download.

When it has been successfully copied to your hard disk, it will start itself and run in the background thus enabling sound files on Web pages to be automatically played.

This is available at no cost from:

```
http://www.real.com/products/player/playerdl.html
```

High levels of IT capability can be developed through the use of the Internet in music education. The Internet can particularly contribute to performing, composing, listening and appraising.

For performing and composing go to:

```
http://www.uce.ac.uk/education/research/music
```

At this site pupils can download a 'midi' file and then add to it in some way, eventually republishing their own version of the work on the site. To achieve this the school will need access to suitable equipment that allows downloaded midi files to be played and changed.

This will require a music sequencing package or a keyboard with a midi file player. It is also possible to create your own music and record it using the facilities available on your computer as most new computers will have a midi frequenting package included in the system. The recorded files can then be inserted into your own Web pages.

For listening and appraising the pupils you will require access to a world library of musical resources, which can be related to a historical and cultural context, by further research on the Web using appropriate research tools (see Part 1, Chapter 2). The comments and music files can be published on a school Intranet.

ART

Introduction

The Web has become a major depository of artwork. In 1996 an electronic art experience residing on the Internet was auctioned on the

Internet for a considerable sum of money. Most of the major art galleries have sites on the Web with examples of work that can be downloaded and there are a considerable number of critiques of works of art published on Web pages.

Activity Art 1 – my Web sketchbook

Teacher notes

National Curriculum	Key Stage 3 General requirements: 2b, 3 Investigating and Making: 7a, 7b, 8a, 8b, 8c
Activity aims	To support research and experimentation with the Web as a resource. To be able to publish on the Web

The use of the sketchbook is fundamental to all art activities. This activity encourages pupils to create their own electronic sketchbook to complement the traditional sketchbook.

Crucial to this activity is the pupils' skills in searching for and downloading graphics items from the Web.

As part of this activity students will be expected to experiment with some of this source material and include it within their electronic sketchbook. Source material will need to be found by using the appropriate search tools (see Part , Chapter 2). Pictures on the Web are normally JPEG or GIF (see Part 1, Chapter 4) image files. Images can be edited in a graphics package such as *Paint Shop Pro* or *JPEG View*.

Pupil activity sheet – my Web sketchbook

The use of a sketchbook is fundamental to all art activities, so we expect you to establish an electronic sketchbook in addition to your normal sketchbook.

It is suggested that you establish the framework for your book in a familiar format such as a Web document. Images for your sketchbook can be found using the search tools that are available to you.

There is a vast collection of images from a great variety of artists published on the Web. These images can be downloaded and stored on disk.

You may want to edit the picture in some way using a graphics package. You could highlight certain areas, crop it, emboss it or experiment with some other changes. Once you are happy with the image, you can save it as a Gif or Jpeg file and transfer it to your Web document.

Activity Art 2 – my net gallery

Teacher notes

National Curriculum	Key Stage 3 General requirements: 5a, 5b, 7e Knowledge and Understanding: 9a, 9b, 9c
Activity aims	To use the Web as a multimedia design and publishing medium

In this activity pupils are expected to examine a site which has been established by various artists as a gallery for their work. The site is an exciting one, with examples of work from modern artists in a variety of different formats. Some of the work involves sound, others involve the moving image. The site is found at:

```
http://www.art.net/the_gallery.html
```

After examining the site pupils are asked to create their own gallery in an electronic format. Initially, they are asked to select a theme for their site and a plan for the gallery. This will mainly involve researching the Web.

Once the theme is decided, pupils will need to start producing and collecting images. If it is decided that display material is required from other sources, access to a scanner and digital camera will be required. At least 30 per cent of the material should be derived from the Web.

The gallery Web pages can be prepared in advance by using a software package such as Microsoft FrontPage or some other suitable Web authoring software (see Part 1, Chapter 3). The finished Web document could be put on to the Web or used on the Intranet in your school.

Pupil activity sheet – my net gallery

You will need access to the Web, a scanner, a digital camera and Web page construction software. The objective of this activity is to maintain or establish a gallery of artwork for your school.

You will first need to design your gallery based on the artwork to which you have access. As most of the art can be stored in an electronic format by either scanning or digital photography, there should be no problems with respect to the quantity of art. You can access the Web for at least 50 per cent of the material in your gallery, but 50 per cent must come from your own group, class or school.

Look at the way in which artists on the Web have designed their gallery at:

```
http://www.art.net/the_gallery.html
```

Note the background they have used and remember that most backgrounds can be captured from the Web. Look at the organization of the gallery and the way in which it has been broken up into smaller sections.

You will need to spend the first ten minutes of this activity deciding on your theme and constructing, on paper, the structure of your gallery. Collect the paintings and other exhibits that you are going to display and prepare them electronically.

Paintings can be scanned, objects can be photographed using a digital camera, and Web images can be transferred to a disk. Bear in mind that some materials are subject to copyright and you may need to ask permission before using them.

It is also important that the electronic images are the right size for your Web gallery as large pictures take a long time to load. It is therefore best to prepare the pictures in two sizes; as a thumbnail and in a size which takes up about a third of a normal sized screen. Make sure that your gallery has at least 12 items in it.

The electronic images can be manipulated using a software package and when ready can be loaded on to Web pages. You will need to make sure that the image has an appropriate title and also think about the presentation of other items on the page such as fonts and backgrounds.

RELIGIOUS EDUCATION

Introduction

It was once said that God was mentioned more times on Web pages than any other noun. When the word was entered into the Alta Vista search engine, it resulted in about two million results.

From the early inception of the Web the Vatican had an extensive site which has now been joined by Muslim, Hindu, Sikh and other faiths. One strength of the Web is that all religions have found a home in its vastness.

This provides opportunities for pupils to have access to up-to-date information on what is happening in other faith communities. The Internet and Web also allows pupils to join discussion groups and send emails which can enhance their ability to communicate with people of different faiths all over the world.

As there are no National Curriculum orders for Religious Education, there are no National Curriculum requirements for Information Technology in Religious Education. There is however some guidelines, published by SCAA (School Curriculum and Assessment Authority) in 1994, which give model syllabuses for Religious Education, and these can be used to guide teachers in the use of the Internet with regard to this curriculum area.

Activity Religious Education I – an Islamic presentation

Teacher notes

> Suitable for Key Stage 3

The Internet allows pupils to collect up-to-date information, in multi-media format, from sites all over the world. Islam is chosen for this activity but any other faith could present similar opportunities.

Pupils will need to be familiar with the search tools (see Part 1, Chapter 2). There is so much information available in this subject area that, for success in this activity, pupils need to be capable of using sophisticated search tools.

For example, typing 'Islam' into a typical search engine resulted in about 800 000 references, so pupils will need to make some thoughtful decisions on what they are looking for so that they can reach the information they require. Entering 'Islam and music' was not as helpful as entering 'Islamic music' but the best results can be obtained by entering '(Islam* and music) and history'. This prevents you from obtaining examples of the more modern Islamic musical structures.

The activity sheet tries to guide pupils but it is still important that the search tool section of this book is consulted, particularly the part on Boolean operators (see Part 1, Chapter 2).

There are two useful sites to start the study at:

```
http://eawc.evansville.edu/ispage.htm
```

and

`http://www.liii.com/~hajeri/islam.html`

The information collected on the Web and from other sources can be electronically published on the pupils' own Web pages. This could then be published on the school Intranet or on the school's Web pages.

There are many kinds of Web authoring package, some especially designed for the younger pupils (see Part 1, Chapter 3). Microsoft FrontPage is an ideal construction tool if the difficult initial structuring of the Web has already been completed. You may need to provide pupils with a template for their Web presentation.

Pupil activity sheet – an Islamic presentation

Your group is to prepare an electronic presentation on Islam. The presentation will be presented as Web pages that will contain text, pictures and sound. It will consist of an initial Home page and should contain links to at least ten other pages. Your teacher will provide the template for your Web presentation.

The first part of the task will be to decide upon the general structure of your Islam site. To do this, you might need to do some initial research on Islam. There is a good introduction to Islam at:

`http://eawc.evansville.edu/ispage.htm`

This and other data should give you enough material to plan the Islam presentation. With a plan you can now do some more research on the Web using the search tools that are available to you. Look for sites that have pictures and examples of Islamic music that you can download.

Collect pictures, text and sound, save them to disk and use these in your presentation. Take care to plan your pages so that they are well designed and easy to read. Ensure that the pictures are not too big and that you do not put too many on any single page.

Index

Index

Index

Index